FRUITFUL

ISOLATION

FRUITFUL
ISOLATION

Billy Strachan

OM Publishing
Bromley, Kent

Biblical quotations are from the New International Version,
© 1973, 1978, 1984 by International Bible Society, published
in Britain by Hodder & Stoughton Ltd; and from the
Authorised Version (Crown copyright)

A catalogue record for this book is available
from the British Library

ISBN 1 85078 092 7

OM Publishing is an imprint of Send The Light
(Operation Mobilisation),
PO Box 48, Bromley, Kent, BR1 3JH, England

Production and Printing in England by
Nuprint Ltd, Station Road, Harpenden, Herts, AL5 4SE.

Dedication

To the one person I know who does not need to read this book to learn the art of Fruitful Isolation—my wife Grace. Down the years she has very faithfully served Christ in unknown isolated ways, supported only by him, in order that I might fulfil the service he commanded of me.

Acknowledgements

Since this is a first, I wish to express my thanks to those who encouraged me to start writing:

To Roger Palms, editor of *Decision* magazine, who walked me in the gardens of Pilgrim Hall in England and told me it was time.

To Christian Larsen of Denmark, who introduced me to computing and word processing.

To Brent Welch, a businessman from Wisconsin, USA, who supplied the computer.

To Danny Jelley of La Grange, Georgia, USA, who nagged and nagged and nagged and nagged until I sat down and began.

A special thanks to my daughter Sandra, who gave the manuscript its first reading and corrected my punctuation and spelling.

Contents

Author's Note

In studying the epistles of Paul over the years of my faith in Christ, I have often wondered how the apostle must have felt as he wrote those now famous letters of his that form part of the New Testament. So in this book I have done the ridiculous and imagined what thoughts and feelings he might have experienced while he dictated his letter to the church in Philippi.

As you read, do remember that much of what I have written is conjecture. But Paul's final text, as we have it today, will appear (usually in the New International Version, NIV) in bold italics throughout the book. This will distinguish the formal epistle, as inspired within Paul by the Holy Spirit, from the informal conversations of Paul and Epaphroditus (his probable secretary), which are my own invention. In addition, to help the reader, each chapter begins with the text of the epistle that is covered in that chapter, printed in both the NIV and the King James Authorised Version (KJV).

One last word. As a Bible school teacher, my aim is not to reveal exactly what I believe, but to teach in a way that might be controversial and even irritating enough to provoke my pupils into getting their Bibles out again after class and searching the word, to come to their own conclusions and crystalise their own beliefs. I have sought to do the same here and apologise in advance for irritating you. I do so with a twinkle in my eye!

Billy Strachan

Prologue

IN THIS MODERN DAY and age, there is a growing
feeling among many Christians who have caught the
vision of the Great Commission, that is, 'Go into all
the world and preach the good news...',[1] that they want
to but cannot because they feel imprisoned. Their
prisons rarely have bars, yet appear to be nonetheless
secure: the prison of a kitchen, an employment, looking
after or being an ill, handicapped or elderly family mem-
ber. It is to prisoners of such situations, those who feel
that they can have no reprieve, that this book is dedi-
cated, as we visit the apostle Paul somewhere in Rome.
Through these pages I hope to show how, by the grace of
God, he tackled such a situation, thereby demonstrating
to us how to rise above these invisible bars.

The sun rose as usual that morning in Rome as it had for
endless centuries. Saul of Tarsus awoke and, as was his
custom, bowed his head and said his morning prayers to
his God and Father, thanking him for another night's
rest and for giving him another day in which to serve his
Lord and Master, Jesus Christ. While his own spirit was
ready and eager to be used by the Holy Spirit that day,

he still had to live within the limits of his ageing body. He rose from his bed and stood once more on those bandy legs of his—legs that made him smaller than most and had brought him the nickname 'Paul', meaning 'the little one'. How he resented that name! He went over to the polished copper that acted as a mirror in his scantily furnished room and checked how much he could see of himself with his failing eyes.[2] But before he could become depressed about these weaknesses, he reminded himself that the Lord had spoken to him about such things before and assured him that *his* grace would be sufficient and that *his* power would be made perfect in weakness.[3] So 'up and at it in the strength of the Lord' had become his daily adage.

Having breakfasted, he crossed to the table that acted as his desk, and after his usual reading of the word of God, and more prayers, he began to search for the parchment on which he noted down all the things he aimed to achieve each day. It was hard work being an apostle and leader in the ever-growing Church, with new groups forming so speedily. He heard a movement and turned to see faithful Epaphroditus, his helper, entering the room. Epaphroditus had been sent to Rome by the church at Philippi to deliver various gifts and to take care of Paul's needs. He had done this diligently and tirelessly, to the point that he had for a time been very ill. Having come through this together, and over the months working and praying together, the two men had become very close friends.[4]

'Ah, Epaphroditus. Just the man I need, and on time as usual. You should have stayed in bed a bit longer this morning. You know how your health has been these days.'

'You can talk! The day you learn to stop driving yourself, I promise to follow your example.'

'There's a big difference,' said Paul. 'You, Lord willing, still have much of life ahead of you but I have so much to do and I'm fast running out of time. If *I* don't get it done, who will?'

With an ironic little smile on his face, Epaphroditus said quietly and firmly, 'I'm sure the Lord knows the answer to that question.'

'Thank you, Epaphroditus! That's all I *don't* need this morning, when I think of all that's to be done—and I might add, be done properly. There's trouble in that church in Galatia again and, oh dear me, another mess in Corinth! And look at the places we've wanted to visit for years. Places we just must get to: the far east, Bythinia, Troas, Mysia and Israel . . . Oh! Israel, Israel; how I wish I could get to you with the gospel. I know that the Lord has the answer, Epaphroditus, but don't forget that his specific will for my life included preaching before the people of Israel.[5] Yet all my efforts for Israel seem to have backfired and I'm not getting any younger . . .'

The conversation was suddenly brought to a halt as the increasingly intrusive scrunch of heavy feet along the street came to an abrupt halt outside Paul's house. Without so much as a knock, the door was flung open and there stood the might of Rome in the form of a centurion with a quarternian of soldiers, all armed.

'Saul of Tarsus, known as Paul the Christian and a leader of that sect, the time has come for your long-awaited hearing before the emperor.'

Paul had waited two years for this day. Now it had come unexpectedly and caught him unprepared. They marched him off and, standing alone before the emperor, he saw the depth of that man's sin as he made his pronouncements on the case and gave his verdict: Paul was to be imprisoned securely until a time known only to the emperor, when he would be taken from the place of detention to be executed by beheading as an enemy of Rome.

Paul was stunned as he was led off by the guard and into the prison, down a seemingly never-ending succession of corridors and steps until finally he was pushed into a cell. He heard the door clang shut behind him. He looked round to see the guard turn the key in the lock. As he faced the door, all he felt capable of doing was to listen to the jingle of the keys as they went off into the distance—then there was only silence. He sat down and depression swept over him as he realised he was no longer a leader, apostle, evangelist, preacher, church-planter, teacher or miracle-worker, but simply another prisoner of Rome, unjustly accused and sentenced to death. The man who once declared that he would rather speak five words in an intelligible language than ten thousand words in a tongue,[6] found himself saying these five forlorn words: '*What use am I now?*'

Paul sat with confusion filling his mind as this question roared through his head and seemed to afflict his whole being. 'Where is God and why is he so mysterious and silent, now of all times? I had such plans for this day to glorify his name and now—nothing.'

And the Lord smiled his loving-kindness silently from his throne...

Dear Reader

Have all your personal plans gone wrong?
Do you feel that you are in a prison?
Is the Lord silent at the moment?
Read on...

Notes

1. Mark 16:15.
2. Based on Galatians 4:15, some Bible scholars believe that Paul suffered from weak or failing eyesight.
3. 2 Cor. 12:9.
4. Phil. 2:25–27; 4:18.
5. Acts 9:15.
6. 1 Cor. 14:19.

1

Boredom or a Beginning?

DAYS HAD PASSED but feelings had remained. With each new dawn, Paul anticipated that this must be *the* day. However, it appeared that the Roman judicial system was in no hurry to carry out the execution. Gradually, as the shock of the sentence eased and life settled into a daily routine, those feelings of confusion and depression—which were very real to him—began to be replaced by a sense of boredom.

As was the custom, Epaphroditus had been allowed to come in daily to bring Paul necessities and to help him out in whatever way he could. He had learned that, the way Paul was feeling, the best thing he could do was to be there regularly but to keep silent and not try to talk Paul out of his deepening emotions. Waiting is often the hardest part of being a Christian. Epaphroditus knew that all too often words can be the source of misunderstanding, especially if spoken too soon. So he prayed silently and constantly, knowing that prayer could move mountains, as it released the activity of God in that prison cell. Paul himself had taught him that man's extremity is God's opportunity. At times he was tempted to shoot the apostle with his own bow and arrow but had the divine prompting within his own heart that, when a man was as low as Paul was, that would be the worst thing he could do.

The waiting finally paid off and in the middle of the morning of an otherwise uneventful day, Paul broke the silence himself.

'It looks like it's not going to be today either.'

Epaphroditus silently prayed on.

'Well, since it appears we may have some time to waste, what can we waste it on?...Epaphroditus?'

'I'm listening.'

'Did I ever write to that church fellowship of yours and thank them for the financial support they sent with you when you first came to see me?'

'As a matter of fact you didn't. You never seemed to find the time for that because of the pressure of your other ministries.'

'Then get some parchment. Let's occupy ourselves and break this boredom by writing some long-overdue letters.'

So began a new experience for Paul in his enforced isolation. As life in the prison cell continued, the boredom of his day was broken. Feelings of depression lifted as he wrote one letter after another, letters that would finally make their way into the New Testament, labelled by Bible students down the ages since as the prison epistles—Philippians, Colossians, Ephesians and Philemon. They were inspired by the Holy Spirit through the mind of Paul during a time of isolation and as an example to us to use some of our 'boring time' to do the same. Who knows but that some letter you write today to break your particular isolation may very well be equally inspired and used by the Lord in your own life to shut off that hobby of most isolationists of just sitting and listening to the constant churning of their own minds?

Human nature being as it is, I can almost hear Paul in heaven right now enquiring of the Lord: 'Who is that down there talking about me, and what letters is he referring to, Lord?'

'The ones, my son, that you wrote while you awaited your execution.'

'Those letters, Lord? How did he get hold of those?'

'They are in the New Testament, Paul.'

'The New Testament, Lord? What's that?'

'That is of no concern to you now, Paul. But, knowing you, had you known that you were writing part of it, you would have been the first to put your foot down and stop it from coming into being. You would have taught that everything new is suspect, that the Law and the Prophets had been good enough to preach from for generations so it would not be necessary to have any modern additions. So I did not consult you, Paul; I just used you in your isolation. I know you thought I had abandoned you because I was silent about it.'

'And people have been reading my letters ever since?'

'Yes, my son.'

'But, Lord, those were personal. You didn't by any chance get that first one I wrote to Timothy, did you?'

'Indeed I did, my son.'

'But I didn't intend that for anyone else's eyes. Had I known you would be letting others read it I would have thought twice about putting in that bit about taking a little wine for his stomach's sake. Was the spelling and grammar all right? Oh, Lord! You surely didn't get hold of the one I wrote to the Galatian churches?'

'Of course, Paul.'

'Oh dear! Let me explain about that one, Lord. I wasn't feeling myself that morning; I was a bit liverish, I think, and had lost my temper. I wasn't quite—how shall I put it?—filled with your Holy Spirit that day.'

'Paul, Paul, Paul. Relax, my son. I assured you right from the start that you were my chosen instrument to carry my name. It was not dependent on how you would feel or what your mood would be. In fact, the one thing I could rely on was your extreme moods of temperament. These allowed me to use you to write to the Galatian Christians and thus pen the finest treatise on how to be free from law and enjoy my grace. It has been the most releasing of all your letters. In fact, one often thinks it might have been better if you had let your feelings loose a bit more often; we might have had some more letters of such value.'

Dear Reader

How do you feel today?

Are you bored?

Is there any activity you could do right now?

Do you prefer self-pity?

Will you 'get on' and trust the Lord's silence?

2

Time to Pray

Philippians 1:1

KJV
Paul and Timotheus, the servants of Jesus Christ, to all the saints in Christ Jesus which are at Philippi, with the bishops and deacons...

NIV
Paul and Timothy, servants of Christ Jesus. To all the saints in Christ Jesus at Philippi, together with the overseers and deacons...

PAUL BEGAN to pace up and down the cell as he gathered his thoughts, while Epaphroditus waited with his reed pen poised over the parchment.

'I suppose we may as well start with the usual formalities, of who is writing and to whom: Paul, to all my converts in my church that I started in Philippi.'

Epaphroditus did not write this and, in his love and respect for this great man of God, kept his face downwards, silently asking the Lord to help him. Then, respectfully but fearfully (for he of all people knew how volatile Paul could be), he asked, 'Do you really want me to put that down?'

'Why? What's wrong with it?' demanded Paul, with a look of amazement on his face. 'It's true, isn't it? Was it not my feet that stepped off the boat at Neapolis and walked the Ignatius Road, cobble by cobble, up hill and down hill in the burning heat to Philippi? Was it not I who led Lydia to Christ and after freeing a young girl from demon possession was dragged into the market-place, tried by the magistrates and thrust into prison? And was it not I...?'

'There were others too,' interrupted Epaphroditus.

'Who?' asked Paul.

'There was Silas, for a start.'

'But he was my assistant.'

'The Lord was there too, Paul. Was he your assistant also?'

Paul stood slightly stunned but, as became his age and character, in all humility he thanked Epaphroditus for bringing him back down to earth. He asked for forgiveness, first of the Lord Jesus and then of his friend. As he was about to open his mouth again, Epaphroditus added meekly, 'And while you're at it, you shouldn't call it *your* church. The Lord is building his church—not you or anyone else.'

'How stupid we humans are, Epaphroditus—or should I say, *I* am. Thank you for being so patient with me. Let's start again: *Paul and Timothy, servants of Christ Jesus...*'

'Why mention Timothy, Paul?'

'Because I may not be around for much longer, so I'd better prepare him to continue. And I can at least by letter prepare them for his coming as Christ's replacement for me... *To all the saints in Christ Jesus at Philippi, together with the overseers* [or bishops] *and deacons...* Bishops and deacons...'—and with that Paul sat down on the bed and began to reminisce. His heart was suddenly filled with a lifting sunshine as he and Epaphroditus started recalling one person after another by name. Sometimes they laughed at the fun they had had with each one, and also wept as Paul remembered the cost and suffering some of them had gone through in their early faith in that pagan, immoral society. 'Do you remember when . . . ?' was repeated often, recalling one's problems and pressures, wondering if another ever got through that and over this and on top of the other.

'I say, my son,' said Paul, 'how about putting that pen down and praying for all those we have remembered?'

With that began a prayer-time that took them through to midday. When they were finished and rose from their knees, Paul said, 'Do you know, I can't remember when we last had a prayer-time like that!'

'We've often been too busy to pray, Paul.'

'Yes, and so eager to preach and shepherd and teach and justify our theological position and our authoritative rule over our charges, that we didn't talk to our Father half enough about them. Who would have thought that by being in an isolated position such as this we would be ushered into this new adventure of spending so much time praying for others, and they don't even know we're doing it. Praise God for something new to do! Epaphroditus, let's do this every morning. Who knows, before I get to heaven I may yet understand a little more what the Lord meant when he stated that we should enter our room, close the door and pray in secret to our Father.'[7]

'Great! Now do you mind if I say a little prayer for this meal before it goes to waste? Let's pray . . .'

Dear Reader

Do you claim your service as your own?

Do you silently pray for others rather than jump at
them with verbal judgement?

Are you gentle in correcting others?

Can you admit that you are wrong to yourself and to
others?

Do you confess your sins?

Are you preparing others to do your work?

How often do you remember and pray for others?

Notes

7. Matt. 6:6.

3

Praying

Philippians 1:2–7

KJV

Grace be unto you, and peace, from God our Father, and from the Lord Jesus Christ.

I thank my God upon every remembrance of you,

Always in every prayer of mine for you all making request with joy,

For your fellowship in the gospel from the first day until now;

Being confident of this very thing, that he which hath begun a good work in you will perform it until the day of Jesus Christ:

Even as it is meet for me to think this of you all, because I have you in my heart; inasmuch as both my bonds, and in the defence and confirmation of the gospel, ye all are partakers of my grace.

NIV

Grace and peace to you from God our Father and the Lord Jesus Christ.

I thank my God every time I remember you. In all my prayers for all of you, I always pray with joy because of your partnership in the gospel from the first day until now, being confident of this, that he who began a good work in you will carry it on to completion until the day of Christ Jesus.

It is right for me to feel this way about all of you, since I have you in my heart; for whether I am in chains or defending and confirming the gospel, all of you share in God's grace with me.

THEY HAD FINISHED eating and no amount of persuasion would make Paul sit down and rest for a while. He insisted on carrying on. 'Where were we with that letter when we got waylaid?' asked Paul.

'We were on your very first sentence, when you sat down and started remembering everyone who crossed your mind,' Epaphroditus said with a smile.

'Well, let's give them a formal greeting and tell them we remembered them all. Put down: *Grace and peace to you from God our Father and the Lord Jesus Christ. I thank my God every time I remember you. In all my prayers for all of you, I always pray with joy because of your partnership in the gospel from the first day until now.*'

He stopped and, looking thoughtfully at his dear friend, said, 'That sounds strange, you know.'

'What does?'

'Thanking God that I can remember them and finding that I can remember them with *joy* for their fellowship. When I look back and think of the heartaches and headaches some of them gave me! Oh, there were some pretty awkward characters among them—stubborn, uncompromising. In fact, I could sum it up by saying that at that time they were a "pain in the neck".'

Epaphroditus laughed. Paul stopped and looked across at him.

'And what, may I ask, is amusing you from those very real and serious comments?'

'The idea that it was *they* who were stubborn, uncompromising and a pain in the neck. Why, Paul, you as a leader were sometimes the biggest pain that any of us had to cope with. Still, you would never have achieved what you have so far if you hadn't had that built-in awkwardness.'

'It must be my Benjamite ancestry.'

'Well, knowing that you're a Benjamite has certainly

helped me to understand you better, Paul. You Benjamites are always prone to extremism; in fact, it's your very extremism that's your gift. It would have been a disaster for us to pray that God would change you into what we had in mind for the temperament of an apostle. I remember reading what Jacob said in his prophetic utterance about Benjamin just before he died, that "Benjamin is a ravenous wolf; in the morning he devours the prey, in the evening he divides the plunder."[8] That warned me that Benjamites should be treated with caution.'

'Thanks for helping me to understand myself better, Epaphroditus, because I've often wished I could be different. Still, I'm glad that Moses reminds us that despite our failings, we have a special place in God's heart—he certainly doesn't keep us at arm's length the way our human friends are tempted to do at times.[9]

'But what you say about us is true. Why, in the days of the judges—when Israel was rife with violence, immorality, violation of people's human rights and political intrigue, with loads of false religions and faith in the one true God thrown in—we Benjamites were very lax about obeying God and possessing our inheritance. But then the next thing was that my forefather, Ehud, who everyone thought was a left-handed misfit and not worth having around, found that his awkwardness was God's built-in gift to him. He slew the unsuspecting King Eglon with such ferocity by his left-handedness that the sword disappeared in at the front and came out at the back. There followed years of revival and freedom for the people of God.[10] However, it didn't last, as the pendulum swung and Israel nearly wiped out the entire tribe for condoning gross immorality.'[11]

'Yes, that's certainly your tribal characteristic, Paul. Why, even your namesake, King Saul, was a man of extremes: either a giant in the nation or hiding among the baggage; telling David, in tears, that he had sinned and wanted to repent and be forgiven or trying to kill him with a spear.'

'When you think of it, friend,' said Paul, 'that was exactly me. One minute I was kneeling with brother Barnabas in union of heart and prayer as the Holy Spirit sorted us out for our ministry to the Gentiles, while the next I was yelling at him to go one way and I would go the other, telling him to take John Mark with him as I didn't want him with me. Huh! I could certainly use Mark now. He would be a great help to me.'

'And the Lord used it, Paul, to get the job done. He took your awkwardness into account. How stupid to think that if a person becomes a child of God it should be evidenced by reversal of his or her temperament. We even try to force God in prayer to change this one or that one when what he wants to do is control his people's differences by his Holy Spirit and make them positive attributes for his purposes.'

'Even my outbursts of anger, Epaphroditus?'

'Yes, even those, Paul.'

'Make a note for me, my friend, to write about that sometime, so we can make certain that the church understands that you don't stop being angry in case you sin, but that under his control it's always better to let it out in little puffs so that we don't sin by going to bed suppressing it all and waking up the next day having added resentment to it.'[12]

After mulling over these thoughts for a while, he said to Epaphroditus, 'Interesting, isn't it, that it took time and being in prison before I could begin to understand myself a bit better, and of course all those we've been remembering with joy for their fellowship? After all, the Lord did use many of them in varied and real ways. I didn't mention their awkwardness in my dictating to you, did I?'

'No.'

'Good, but we'll have to tell them to let God use their temperament. In fact, put this down: *...being confident of this, that he who began a good work in you will carry it on to completion until the day of Christ Jesus. It is right for me to feel this way about all of you, since I have you in my heart; for whether I am in chains or defending and confirming the gospel, all of you share in God's grace with me.* What he has done for *this* awkward character, he will do for them all.'

Dear Reader

Who do you remember with joy?

Were *they* the awkward ones or were *you*?

Do you wish you could be someone else instead of the unique 'you' whom God made?

Do you believe that God can use you in spite of yourself?

Notes

8. Gen. 49:27.
9. Deut. 33:12
10. Judges 3:12–30.
11. Judges 19 and 20.
12. Eph. 4:26.

4

The Priorities

Philippians 1:8–11

KJV

For God is my record, how greatly I long after you all in the bowels of Jesus Christ.

And this I pray, that your love may abound yet more and more in knowledge and in all judgement;

That ye may approve things that are excellent; that ye may be sincere and without offence till the day of Christ;

Being filled with the fruits of righteousness, which are by Jesus Christ, unto the glory and praise of God.

NIV

God can testify how I long for all of you with the affection of Christ Jesus.

And this is my prayer: that your love may abound more and more in knowledge and depth of insight, so that you may be able to discern what is best and may be pure and blameless until the day of Christ, filled with the fruit of righteousness that comes through Jesus Christ—to the glory and praise of God.

HAVING SAID THAT, Paul stopped, his eyes filled with tears and he let out a groan that caused Epaphroditus to look up in concern. Finally Paul, wiping his sleeve across his eyes, said: 'Write down: *God can testify how I long for all of you with the affection of Christ Jesus. And this is my prayer* ... Prayer! There are so many things I should pray for them, it would take pages to list them all. One thing is certain, we should start with the priority—love. Put it down that I pray *that your love may abound more and more...*'

'Do you mean that you pray that their efforts at loving should increase, Paul?'

'No, that's not what I mean, brother. Too often we *try* and love; when we take that route, we haven't understood love at all. We can't manufacture love; we have to understand that the Lord is all love and that when we received him into our hearts by faith, he came in by his Spirit and *he is love*. We already possess the love of God, poured into our hearts by the Holy Spirit.[13] What I'm praying for is that *God's love* in our Philippian brothers and sisters will abound, or have more release through them from day to day. No, Epaphroditus, I'm praying that their knowledge of this great truth will increase and while I'm at it, phrase it this way, that I hope their sense of discernment will increase. So say: ...*in knowledge and depth of insight, so that you may be able to discern what is best...* In fact, let's state it stronger still, that they might have a faith that is combined with common sense.'

'I'm glad you said that, Paul.'

'Why?'

'Well, there's so much confusion among church members today. For example, so often people are focussing on the gifts of the Holy Spirit in their lives and making the mistake of picking out their favourite gift and setting it up as the criterion for being a super-believer. Yet in that list of gifts is the gift of discernment, and so few seem to have that gift or even ask for it.'

'Yes indeed, what a difference it would make in all the fellowships if each one had a committed believer sitting in the meetings who could be relied upon to discern when any false teaching had entered the church. Too many, I'm afraid, evaluate spiritual life on the basis of outward, observable behaviourisms and words—there's too much pretence around.'

'You mean play-acting?'

'Yes, and we all know the word for that, don't we? It's hypocrisy. So, Epaphroditus, let's tell them that we are praying for them concerning that matter. Continue writing: ... *that you may be able to discern what is best and may be* ... How shall I describe this? Ah! I have it, Epaphroditus. Describe it in Latin—write *sine ceres* [sincere]. That will get it across to them.'

'But translated, Paul, that means "without wax". How will that help?'

'Because it's the latest phrase that everyone's using. I heard one shopkeeper use it in the market-place in Corinth when I was there. I asked him what it meant and he explained.

'You see, at that time everyone was falling over themselves trying to buy one of those Greek statues for their garden or house, but they were so expensive—since the best marble has to be bought in Italy—that most of them found it beyond their reach. However, one smart fellow got a piece of flawed marble and sculpted a statue as best he could. It was the figure of a burly naked man, and it looked pretty good. The only problem was that the tip of the nose was missing, there was a great gash on one thigh and a bit of one heel had fallen off. But he wouldn't be beaten. He melted white candle wax and moulded a nose tip, filled in the crack and stuck on a heel, and the faults couldn't be detected.

'He perfected this technique and people began to buy his works. They were very happy with them, delighted to show off their latest acquisition to their neighbours. All went well until it got colder and they turned the heat on. When that happened all the wax ran out of the indoor statues and they discovered they had a phony on their hands. They had been tricked.'

'Are you saying, Paul, that a Christian has to be prepared to be seen with no cover-up—all the cracks showing?'

'Exactly, my friend. Just think of the hope that would give to those who have not yet turned to Christ as their Saviour, if they could see that Christians are as weak as they are. It would help them understand that their salvation isn't a reward for being ever so good and law-keeping, but is a gift from God solely on the basis of what the Lord Jesus Christ has done for them in dying on the cross for their sin. Why, people would flock to Christ if they could only grasp what was being offered—*his* life in exchange for theirs!

'It's such a contrast with other religions that are all based on people having to perfect themselves according to the rules of their so-called faiths, right up to the point of death, in the futile hope that they might meet their god in the afterlife. But Christianity is God himself coming out of eternity *now* and coming into sinful lives *now* while people are still bad, and empowering them to change their behaviour, rather than a do-it-by-yourself system.

'Oh, and you can add to my prayer, Epaphroditus, that they should maintain that sincerity, so that no one can find fault with them, right up to the day when Jesus Christ comes back to this earth or calls them home to heaven. Put: ...*and may be pure and blameless until the day of Christ*... And tell them that if they want to be filled, my prayer is that they will be...*filled* (continually)—not with the wax of hypocrisy or pretence, but—*with the fruit of righteousness that comes through Jesus Christ*—for only he can release this fruit in them anyway. That is the sure way to bring forth fruit—*to the glory and praise of God.*'

'I wish you wouldn't get so carried away and go so fast, Paul. I had a hard time getting all that down.'

'You mean you found that hard to swallow, my son!'

'No, Paul—down on the parchment.'

With that they both said 'Amen' and smiled at each other. Unbeknown to them, had they been able to hear it, the Lord said 'Amen' and smiled too!

Dear Reader

What's your love source?

Does your faith make common sense?

Are you able to discern the true from the false?

Are you a wax job?

Is the fruit of Christ's righteousness evident in your
   life?

Notes

13. Rom. 5:5.

5

A New Discovery

Philippians 1:12–18

KJV

But I would ye should understand, brethren, that the things which happened unto me have fallen out rather unto the furtherance of the gospel;

So that my bonds in Christ are manifest in all the palace, and in all other places;

And many of the brethren in the Lord, waxing confident by my bonds, are much more bold to speak the word without fear.

Some indeed preach Christ even of envy and strife; and some also of good will:

The one preach Christ of contention, not sincerely, supposing to add affliction to my bonds:

But the other of love, knowing that I am set for the defence of the gospel.

What then? notwithstanding, every way, whether in pretence or in truth, Christ is preached; and I therein do rejoice, yea, and will rejoice.

NIV

Now I want you to know, brothers, that what has happened to me has really served to advance the gospel. As a result, it has become clear throughout the whole palace guard and to everyone else that I am in chains for Christ. Because of my chains, most of the brothers in the Lord have been encouraged to speak the word of God more courageously and fearlessly.

It is true that some preach Christ out of envy and rivalry, but

*others out of goodwill. The latter do so in love, knowing that I
am put here for the defence of the gospel. The former preach
Christ out of selfish ambition, not sincerely, supposing that they
can stir up trouble for me while I am in chains. But what does it
matter? The important thing is that in every way, whether from
false motives or true, Christ is preached. And because of this I
rejoice.*

Yes, and I will continue to rejoice ...

PAUL WAS JUST about to continue when he heard
that familiar jingle of keys, indicating the
approach of the jailer. That always made him stop
whatever he was doing, for he never knew if it was his
time at last or some other interruption. Being as human
as anyone, to Paul the anticipation of death was always
more alarming than the one step that it would take to
pass into the presence of the Lord. He turned and faced
the door.

'There's more than one pair of feet, Paul,' said
Epaphroditus quietly.

'I know, my friend; with my eyes failing, my ears can
hear more than I have ever heard before, so I heard
them before you did.'

The noise grew louder and at last the jailer appeared.
To their pleasure and surprise, he was followed by
Aristobulus, Persis and Rufus, who were hard on his
heels. Paul in particular was delighted to see these three
dear friends from the church, having been kept from
their company for so long. The jailer ushered them in
and stationed himself at the door. There was the usual
hustle and bustle of their greeting one another.

'Now then,' said Paul, 'this is a surprise! And for what
purpose is this unexpected visit?'

Persis was the first to speak. She was a believer whom
Paul had always regarded with much love, and she had

been such a dependable Christian who worked hard for the Lord's sake.[14]

'Pastor Paul, we have a problem in the church.'

'That's new!' said Paul, with a touch of the sarcasm that he sometimes struggled to keep under control. 'This is the reason for your visit?'

'Yes,' said Aristobulus. 'We felt that you might be able to help us.'

'Friends, as long as I'm alive and accessible I will always try and help where I can but you'd better get used to taking the problems to the Lord in prayer, for I may not be around too much longer. He, however, will always be with you and is far more reliable than I will ever be.'

'Of course we've prayed about this problem, Paul, but we still felt we ought to consult you.'

'So what is the problem?'

'Well, when you suddenly left us, it caused no end of concern to the church.'

'Why?' asked Paul.

'Well, for one thing, you were due to speak at the services that following Lord's day. Everyone was stunned. It was Rufus here who reminded us that you were expected to speak and asked who was going to take your place. That was our first problem because we'd become so used to you, the leader, doing it all, and we were so enjoying your talks on the holiness of God. Knowing how long it was taking you to get through it, we felt certain it would take another month or two and had never anticipated that it would all come to an end so suddenly.'

'So what did you do?' interposed Epaphroditus.

'Well, after a lot of discussion as to who would be the best speaker to replace you, Pastor Paul, it became very evident to us that we couldn't find anyone of your calibre that we could invite. Even Priscilla and Aquila were out of town. We felt we had no alternative but to cancel the meetings, when old Andronicus said *he* would do it.'[15]

'Well, we couldn't allow that, Paul,' said Persis. 'He's getting beyond it now and tends to wander. Besides, he doesn't appeal to the young people any more.'

Aristobulus went on: 'So finally Hermas said that he would have a go.'[16]

'That caused no end of discussion,' said Rufus, 'for he'd never done it before. He hasn't had any real training yet, and his mannerisms are not all very pleasant. Nevertheless, since time ran out on us and the Lord seemed to be silent about the whole thing, we let him go ahead.'

'What happened?' asked Paul. 'Was he any good?'

'Good?' said Rufus. 'He was marvellous and the Lord greatly blessed the gathering through his teaching. It's *since* then that things have heated up.'

'What do you mean?'

'Well, as days have turned into weeks and it's become evident that you might not be coming back, they're *all* having a go and quite a number have found that they've been sitting on a gift of preaching and didn't know it. Now it's like a contest and they're all competing against each other in the hope that maybe if you don't get back, one of them might be the next pastor.'

'In fact,' said Persis, 'I overheard someone say he hoped you might never get back! That's what finally did it and we felt you had to help us because loyalty to you is being affected. It's the talk of Caesar's palace. In fact, the whole city is talking about it and some are even laughing at us.'

'And on top of that,' said Rufus, 'some are blaming the Lord for letting you suffer in jail and not getting you out. Others are suggesting that the Lord is punishing you for some unconfessed sin, while yet others are arguing that it's for your faithful defence of the gospel that you are where you are and...Well, we want to know what you want us to do about it.'

Silence enveloped the small group of believers and Epaphroditus, as was his habit, sat and silently prayed that the Lord would grant Paul grace and wisdom.

'Nothing,' said Paul finally.

The rest, dismay etching their faces, exclaimed, 'Nothing?'

'Nothing at all. What does it matter? I'm overjoyed to discover that my being stuck in here has led you to find your own feet. Why, you're telling me that people are preaching who have never preached before and some are finding that they have had gifts from the Holy Spirit but never used them. Friends, your news excites me and I'm *glad* that I'm in this prison, for it's obvious that I held on too long and had almost taken the place of the Lord in your fellowship.'

Then, with a choked expression and eyes full of tears, he went on to say in a whisper, 'And I hope that, if the result is that others begin to serve the Lord, I don't get out.'

With that, he turned and faced the window, then sat down and sobbed. The others stood there not knowing how to console him. At last Epaphroditus rose from the table and said gently, 'I think perhaps you should leave us now. Go back to the fellowship and remind them that the Lord Jesus is all that any of us need.'

He indicated to the jailer, who then escorted them out and locked the door again. Their footfalls seemed to wander off into the distance, accompanied by those still-jingling keys.

Epaphroditus sat down again, picked up the pen and said, as though the visitors had never been there at all,

'What were you going to say next to the Christians at my church in Philippi, Paul?'

Without so much as a turn of his head he dictated the following without a stop for further comment: *'Now I want you to know, brothers, that what has happened to me has really served to advance the gospel. As a result, it has become clear throughout the whole palace guard and to everyone else that I am in chains for Christ. Because of my chains, most of the brothers in the Lord have been encouraged to speak the word of God more courageously and fearlessly. It is true that some preach Christ out of envy and rivalry, but others out of goodwill. The latter do so in love, knowing that I am put here for the defence of the gospel. The former preach Christ out of selfish ambition, not sincerely, supposing that they can stir up trouble for me while I am in chains. But what does it matter? The important thing is that in every way, whether from false motives or true, Christ is preached. And because of this I rejoice. Yes, and I will continue to rejoice...*

'What does it matter, what does it matter, Epaphroditus?' exclaimed Paul, tears still running down his face and yet his eyes alight with joy. 'What a great new discovery, that for me to be in isolation is the Lord's way of releasing others into the same work he gave me. Let Rome take my head; I am not finished for *he* is not finished. The Lord will always replace one with many more for he will not be defeated by the powers of this world.'

They looked at each other and, with a unity that the world and even some Christians might not understand, they stretched out their hands and held each other in a long embrace of soul, saying in unison, 'What does it matter!'

Dear Reader

Are you ever in a panic when today goes wrong?

What do you look for in people?

Do you ever blame God for the chaos you see around you?

Have you any 'gifts' that you have never used?

What does it matter to you?

Notes

14. Rom. 16:12.
15. Rom. 16:7.
16. Rom. 16:14.

6

Love Keeps Hope Alive

Philippians 1:19–26

KJV

For I know that this shall turn to my salvation through your prayer, and the supply of the Spirit of Jesus Christ.

According to my earnest expectation and my hope, that in nothing I shall be ashamed, but that with all boldness, as always, so now also Christ shall be magnified in my body, whether it be by life, or by death.

For to me to live is Christ, and to die is gain.

But if I live in the flesh, this is the fruit of my labour: yet what I shall choose I wot not.

For I am in a strait betwixt two, having a desire to depart, and to be with Christ; which is far better:

Nevertheless to abide in the flesh is more needful for you.

And having this confidence, I know that I shall abide and continue with you all for your furtherance and joy of faith;

That your rejoicing may be more abundant in Jesus Christ for me by my coming to you again.

NIV

. . . for I know that through your prayers and the help given by the Spirit of Jesus Christ, what has happened to me will turn out for my deliverance. I eagerly expect and hope that I will in no way be ashamed, but will have sufficient courage so that now as always Christ will be exalted in my body, whether by life or by death. For to me, to live is Christ and to die is gain. If I am to go on living in the body, this will mean fruitful labour for me. Yet

what shall I choose? I do not know! I am torn between the two: I desire to depart and be with Christ, which is better by far; but it is more necessary for you that I remain in the body. Convinced of this, I know that I will remain, and I will continue with all of you for your progress and joy in the faith, so that through my being with you again your joy in Christ Jesus will overflow on account of me.

W HEN PAUL had finally regained his composure, he turned for a while to what he could see of the blue sky through the tiny barred window. Epaphroditus crossed the room and sat again before the parchment. Paul turned, looked at Epaphroditus and said, 'Do you think it would be too selfish if I were to ask the Christians in your church at Philippi to pray for one request for me while I'm in this place, my brother?'

'Paul, it's been a long time since I heard you ask for something for yourself. You've spent all your prayer time as a pastor praying for others, and the others always felt that that was what you were there for. In fact, I can't recall a prayer meeting being instituted on a regular basis for you, the pastor. Most people imagine you to be so close to God that you don't need it.'

'Then let's put my prayer need down.'

Epaphroditus gave him time to form the request, then obediently recorded it as Paul went on in his dictation: '*...for I know that through your prayers and the help given by the Spirit of Jesus Christ, what has happened to me will turn out for my deliverance.*'

The pen stopped scratching so suddenly that Paul turned and peered at Epaphroditus.

'What's the matter—run out of ink?'

'No, I was wondering why you referred to the Holy Spirit as the Spirit of Jesus. I mean, haven't you always said that there's a Trinity in the Godhead?'

'Yes, of course, my son. If you read the word of God

as you would an atlas, you can come to no other conclusion but that there's a Trinity. Do you get my meaning?'

'No, not quite.'

'Well, if you look at an atlas of Caesar's empire, no matter which part you look at you must notice that, like spokes of a wheel, all major roads lead to a place called Rome. Any stranger in a far-flung part, getting a look at an atlas for the first time, must conclude, in seeing the name Rome so often, that it must indeed be a place, for it's on the map. So with the Trinity; from the beginning of the Scriptures and throughout God's word the Trinity is on the map, even if you don't fully understand it. The problem arises when we, with our finite minds, think that we can understand the infinite meaning. We cannot; however, the Trinity is still on the map, so to speak. Jesus himself referred to the triune nature of the Godhead. His own words were, "I..."—in other words, *the Son*—"...will ask *the Father*, and he will give you another Counsellor to be with you for ever—*the Spirit* of truth. The world cannot accept him, because it neither sees him nor knows him. But you know him, for he lives with you and will be in you..."—referring to the Spirit's coming at Pentecost. "I will not leave you as orphans; I will come to you. Before long the world will not see me any more, but you will see me. Because I live, you also will live. On that day you will realise that I am in my Father, and you are in me, and I am in you.... My Father will love him..."—any believer in the Lord Jesus Christ—"...and *we* will come to him and make our home with him" '[17]

He stopped and looked at Epaphroditus.

'Are you still with me?'

'I think so.'

'The cry of Israel is right, Epaphroditus—"Hear, O Israel: The Lord our God, the Lord is one."[18] Yet for our help the word shows us our God as a Father in heaven and as a Son while here in a physical body prepared by God, the Spirit of holiness, in the womb of Mary, and as God the Spirit of holiness who is everywhere. However, we mustn't fall into the trap of thinking that there are three separate deities. Always remember, God is a Trinity, three in one. Therefore, to refer to the Holy Spirit as the Spirit of Jesus Christ is quite in order. Now do you get it?'

'No, but I did get the fact that I am finite and with a brain like mine and as human as I am, I'll conclude that I have a lot of learning yet to do. I'll therefore rather underestimate my intelligence, give God and his word the winning place and wait. I'm sure he will show me clearly one day. One thing is certain, Paul: I may not fully understand the Godhead, but it's of no consequence, for I know enough of the working of the Lord in my life to know that God is there and doing great things for me. I'll keep enjoying his work in my life and let the understanding slip by me for the present.'

'Then let's continue, shall we?... *I eagerly expect and hope that I will in no way be ashamed*... It's a very real fear I've always had, my brother, that I would end up being such an old drop-out that God would have to put me aside from the ministry.[19] If I were to drop out, all those who look in my direction and have hope encouraged in them by his ability to keep me, would end up losing hope because they may simply conclude that if the Lord has run out of "steam" to keep me, the apostle, then there will be no "steam" for them. They might therefore give up, giving the enemy victory. It was never beginning with Christ that worried me; it's always been a fear that as I near the end of the race, I might stumble and fall and be so ashamed. Oh! I hope they will pray for me, Epaphroditus, in this matter. Say: ... *but will have sufficient courage so that now*—while I'm in isolation—*as always Christ will be exalted in my body, whether by life or by death*... Have you ever looked through one of those pieces of glass that magnifies things?'

'Yes. Someone showed me one the other day, Paul.'

'What conclusions did you come to?'

'They're good for making the invisible visible and the distant nearer.'

'Exactly! The first time I saw something through one, what jumped into my mind was what Dr Luke told us of Mary when she visited her cousin Elizabeth and burst out into song with, "My soul doth magnify the Lord, and my spirit hath rejoiced in God my Saviour."[20] She had insight into the deep things of God. The words were simply explaining how her mind, will and emotions, and her body also, magnified the Lord. For no man has seen God at any time, but she was the first to be a "magnifying glass" for God in making him visible and nearer. That's what I want in these closing days, Epaphroditus. Whether I'm out there again in freedom or even if I never get out again, that in every way my mind, will and emotions, and body too, will always make him visible to others and nearer to them.'

'I learned something else with the one I looked through the other day, Paul.'

'What was that?'

'I was looking at a little boy's nose through the glass and commented on how big his nose had become, and he just laughed and said, "I see yours is big, too, from my side." It's a two-way action, Paul. The Lord is not only magnified by us as we become his magnifying glasses, but we become bigger too.'

'Why, of course, and we should not be surprised at that because the word has already declared that. We're told in the Scriptures that God magnified both Joshua[21] and Solomon.'[22]

'Yes and David, too, encouraged us in the Psalms[23] to magnify the Lord with him.'

'I hope I can be a good magnifying glass in these difficult days, whether I live or have to magnify him in my death. Put this down in the letter: *For to me, to live is Christ and to die is gain. If I am to go on living in the body, this will mean fruitful labour for me*—to magnify him here in this prison to all who come here, from the jailer and lawyers to the cooks and toilet cleaners; yes, even to Nero himself. *Yet what shall I choose? I do not know! I am torn between the two: I desire to depart*—and get out of this prison, as well as the prison of this ageing, tired body—*and be with Christ, which is better by far; but it is more necessary for you that I remain in the body. Convinced of this*...'

'That makes you sound full of confidence, Paul. I thought you always advocated that we were not to have confidence...'

'Truly, brother, natural, human confidence is self-confidence and is determined by a reliance on ourselves, and that's always wrong. I told the Corinthians, "Not that we are competent [sufficient] in ourselves to claim anything for ourselves, but our competence comes from God."[24] But this confidence I now speak of is confidence in the Lord's ability to keep me, for he loves me and his love for me and my love for him keep my hope alive. So put it down and don't argue with my heart and hope: *Convinced of this, I know that I will remain, and I will continue with all of you for your progress and joy in the faith, so that through my being with you again your joy in Christ Jesus will overflow on account of me.*'

'I admire your hope, Paul, but what if you don't get out again?'

'I will get out of here, Epaphroditus—dead or alive.

Remember what I've already stated: "Love always hopes...";[25] especially when, humanly speaking, there's nothing left to hope for and, as I've further said, when all else is gone there will be three things left—faith, hope and love.[26] So, in the face of the ridiculousness of my present imprisonment, I persist because I have three things left and one of them is *hope*. I shall hope to the end no matter what happens.'

'There it is again, Paul.'

'There's what again?'

'What does it matter?'

Dear Reader

Do you feel that God has finished with you?

Do you simply enjoy the fullness of the Godhead in you or are you trying too hard to understand God?

What kind of magnifying glass are you?

Do you still hope although, humanly speaking, the situation is hopeless?

Notes

17. John 14:16–20,23b.
18. Deut. 6:4.
19. 1 Cor. 9:27.
20. Luke 1:46,47, KJV.
21. Josh. 4:14, KJV.
22. 1 Chron. 29:25, KJV.
23. Ps. 34:2.
24. 2 Cor. 3:5.
25. 1 Cor. 13:7.
26. 1 Cor. 13:13.

7

Behave Yourself

Philippians 1:27,28

KJV
Only let your conversation be as it becometh the gospel of Christ: that whether I come and see you, or else be absent, I may hear of your affairs, that ye stand fast in one spirit, with one mind striving together for the faith of the gospel;

And in nothing terrified by your adversaries: which is to them an evident token of perdition, but to you of salvation, and that of God.

NIV
Whatever happens, conduct yourselves in a manner worthy of the gospel of Christ. Then, whether I come and see you or only hear about you in my absence, I will know that you stand firm in one spirit, contending as one man for the faith of the gospel without being frightened in any way by those who oppose you. This is a sign to them that they will be destroyed, but that you will be saved—and that by God.

PAUL PAUSED with a questioning look on his brow as he studied his friend's face, expecting him to say more, but Epaphroditus just returned his gaze. Finally Paul said, 'So! What *does* it matter? I might get back to them once more or I might not.'

'Yes, but if you leave it just like that in the letter, they could misinterpret it and sit back and do nothing. They might allow a backlog of all sorts of problems, questions and practical issues to pile up, in the hope that you may return to sort the whole mess out.'

'Point taken, Epaphroditus. Then say this: *Whatever happens, conduct yourselves in a manner worthy of the gospel of Christ. Then, whether I come and see you or only hear about you in my absence, I will know that you stand firm in one spirit...*'

'Do you mean the Holy Spirit?'

'No, not this time; I mean their own spirit. Remember that man is a tripartite being: spirit, soul and body.[27] God intended that our spirit, indwelt by the Holy Spirit, should control and direct our soul, and through our soul, our body. The soul is the self, comprising the will, the mind or intellect and the emotions.'

'Did you think that out by yourself, Paul?'

'Not at all. It comes straight from God's word. Remember your Torah, the section that most people skip over because it's all about building the tabernacle. It's in just such parts of his word that God in his wisdom places truths that will be found by those who seek him with their whole heart. You'll notice there an instruction from the Lord to Moses to take up an offering from "whosoever is of a willing *heart*".[28] Since heart and soul can be interchangeable words in Scripture, this indicates that the soul contains man's capacity to exercise his free *will* ...'

'Do we really have a free will?'

'Of course we do. If we didn't we wouldn't be in the image of God, for he, to be God, must be free. If we don't have that attribute, we're not in his image and would be mere puppet creatures, only capable of movement as God moves us.'

'Some Christians already believe that anyway, Paul.'

'Yes, I know. That's why they passively sit round thinking they're spiritual, waiting to be mystically moved by God. They seem to think that being spiritual means by-passing the mind and body, overlooking the fact that God is concerned with every part of us; after all, he requires that we use our whole being to love him.[29] Now you'll note also that it tells us the further content of the soul when it states, "And every wise hearted among you..."[30] The soul is the seat of man's intelligence, his *mind*, which thinks and reasons. Lastly, you'll see the third content of the soul when you read: "whose heart stirred him up";[31] in other words, *emotion.*'

'Did the Lord ever mention these things?'

'He certainly did. I remember John Mark telling me of an incident that Peter had told him about. Jesus had allowed some men to break up the roof of a home in Capernaum to lower a paralytic man down before him for healing, and he had told him that his sins were forgiven. Some of the teachers of the law who witnessed this were thinking to themselves that only God could forgive sins, and immediately Jesus, knowing in his own spirit that they were thinking like that, said to them, "Why reason ye these things in your hearts?"[32] That was Jesus confirming that the *mind* is within the heart, or soul.

'Later, right after he had let poor confused Peter know what a failure he'd be, he said to him and the other disciples, "Do not let your hearts be troubled..."[33] So in that statement he was giving credence to the soul being the seat of *emotion*, for fear and worry are emotions. Again, when the Jews were arguing with him, John mentioned that Jesus told them they were for ever searching the Scriptures because it was by them that they thought they had eternal life. It was those very Scriptures, which they emotionally loved and intellectually thought about, that testified of him, but their problem was that they would not exercise their *wills* to come to him.'[34]

'I understand that, Paul—I think! But what about this human *spirit* you started off with? So far you've just spoken about the soul.'

'If you would only listen and stop interrupting me I would get to it. Go back to the passage "whose heart stirred him up" and you'll note that I was about to quote the next phrase, "and every one whom his *spirit* made willing".[35] You see, the practical actions taken by the mind, will and emotions are motivated by the human spirit. God gave us our spirit so that we could be in communion with him. We can understand about God with our mind but we can only truly *know* him with our spirit. At the fall, man's spirit died, in the sense that it was cut off from God. Every human being since Adam and Eve has been born in this condition; we are separated from God and therefore lack the presence and power of God within our spirits to control our behaviour. That was certainly my problem. My godless *spirit* was always driving my behaviour to such an extent that when I came across the first Christians, I persecuted them and even assisted at the martyrdom of Stephen, my brother in Christ. I thank God that he long ago forgave me for that—as did Stephen with his dying breath—and healed the sting of the memory. But of course I still remember what I did...'

He paced up and down as he spoke, but before he could get caught up too deeply in that memory, he gave himself a shake and continued.

'A good example of human spirit activity, Epaphroditus, was Apollos. Remember the confusion he caused when he first went to Ephesus? He had heard the preaching of John the Baptist as he travelled from Alexandria up through Israel to Greece and had been so caught up with John's message, which had so evidently affected him that, being an excellent public speaker, he preached and taught about Jesus accurately, but in the liveliness of his *own* spirit, not the Holy Spirit.

'Yet John had only preached repentance and a baptism by water for the remission of sins and had told everyone that his preaching was not enough and that there would be one coming after him, namely the Lord Jesus. He would not simply give people forgiveness and a new start, but forgiveness and a new *life*; in fact his very self inside their spirits by the Holy Spirit. It was Priscilla and Aquila who sorted Apollos out. After that his message changed and he began preaching about the Lord Jesus in the power of the Holy Spirit.'[36]

'I see.'

'Then get that pen and write what I was saying: *I will know that you stand firm in one spirit*—that is, as true *spirit*-directed people made in the image of God, they should be unified in their determination to rely upon his life within them to demonstrate, more than by preaching and attending meetings, a behaviour that speaks louder than anything else.'

'But if what you're saying is true, Paul, it means that although Christians are indwelt by the Holy Spirit, their renewed human spirit has to come into action and co-operate with the Holy Spirit in a practical way before the Lord's life can be released through them.'

'Good lad! You're getting there. That's why I've always been at pains to tell believers not to quench[37] or grieve[38] the Holy Spirit. In so doing, although he will still be present, we will hinder his activity in our lives. So much so-called spiritual activity is in fact our own selfish-spirit activity, a misuse of the equipment that the Lord has given us for his use; it shows that we're not yet yielded to his control. Worse still perhaps, our thoughts and actions can descend to the worldly or carnal level. When we allow the soul to take control, it leads to behaviour such as jealousy and quarrelling.[39] As soon as we detect this taking place we should climb down and admit that it is of self, one way or another. Blaming the demon spirit world or claiming that we couldn't help what was happening because the Holy Spirit was making us do it is simply nonsense. In the case of the gifts of the Holy Spirit, the spirits of those exercising the gift in question, be it prophecy, speaking in tongues or whatever, are subject to *their* control, for God is not a God of disorder.[40] But if in our spirit we take the lead from *his* Spirit within, and keep our soul in its proper place, we can utilise our own spirit-drive and correctly exercise in our behaviour the gifts he has given us.'

'You mean the gifts the Lord has given can be misused by us and are not always an indication that he is in control and that we're "filled with the Holy Spirit"?'

'Exactly. Now write further: ... *contending as one man*— their *spirits* in unity with the Holy Spirit within each of them—*for the faith of the gospel; without being frightened in any way by those who oppose you. This is a sign to them that they will be destroyed*—awareness that they are lost and don't have that life within their *spirits* that they evidence in your good behaviour—*but that you*—an evidence of that life within you—*will be saved—and that by God*. Oh, what a tremendous testimony they would bear if they would only behave themselves.'

Dear Reader

How do you react?

Do you offer the parts of your body as instruments of righteousness?

Are you practical or mystical?

Do you quench or grieve his Spirit within?

Are his gifts to you misused?

Notes

27. 1 Thess. 5:13.
28. Exod. 35:5, KJV.
29. Mark 12:30; Deut. 6:5.
30. Exod. 35:10, KJV.
31. Exod. 35:21, KJV.
32. Mark 2:6–8, KJV.
33. John 14:1.
34. John 5:39,40.
35. Exod. 35:21, KJV.
36. Acts 18:24–28.
37. 1 Thess. 5:19.
38. Eph. 4:30.
39. 2 Cor. 3:1–3.
40. 1 Cor. 14:32,33.

8

Believe to Suffer

Philippians 1:29

KJV
For unto you it is given in the behalf of Christ, not only to believe on him, but also to suffer for his sake...

NIV
For it has been granted to you on behalf of Christ not only to believe on him, but also to suffer for him...

A S EPAPHRODITUS rolled out more of his parchment and wiped off the point of his pen he asked, 'Why, all of a sudden, did you bring those who oppose us into your thoughts?'

'Because godly behaviour is often very intimidating. It was so in the life of Christ, and he himself said that it would be so in his followers. Remember, John tells us that once when the Lord Jesus was praying to his Father in heaven, he said of his own, "I have given them your word and the world has hated them, for they are not of the world any more than I am of the world."[41]

'What do you think it was that infuriated me about Stephen? That he was a believer in the Lord Jesus Christ? No, a thousand times, no! It was because, although I had spent a lifetime studying Scripture and God as religiously as I could, in order to get through to

God and be accepted by him—and I felt I was doing rather well—I came across an everyday common man whose behaviour in life was, quite simply, godly. And I hated him because of it. At the same time I found out that my years of being meticulously religious had not changed my fallen nature, the rebel within me, one iota—and I killed him. I threw in my vote with the rest of them and cared more for the clothes[42] of the rabble that I incited to do my dirty work than for Stephen, so that I could remain in my own eyes a man who could say to the Almighty, "I have never killed."

'Epaphroditus, do you know that when the discovery of the Lord on the road to Damascus blinded me and I was led into the city to await the arrival of Ananias to open my eyes again,[43] there was one image I saw inside my mind all those days of waiting...and you're the first I've ever told this to in all these years?'

'What was that, Paul?'

'Stephen.'

'Stephen?'

'Yes, Stephen, kneeling down, as one stone after another smashed and bruised him until he was dead. He behaved like a gentleman to the end and I've seen the smile of rest that was on his dying face ever since.'

'You'll see it in reality, Paul, when you meet him in eternity. I'll guarantee that the smile won't have changed, but it will have additional behaviour added—he'll have his arms wide open to hug you.'

Paul wept; Epaphroditus waited. After a while Paul began again.

'So I think it's important to let the Philippian Christians know that the minute they allow the new life of Christ within them to be demonstrated through them in godly behaviour, it will intimidate people—especially religious do-gooders trying to earn their way to heaven.

I've explained this to Timothy and now I must do so to the Philippian believers.[44] Write this down for me: *For it has been granted to you on behalf of Christ not only to believe on him, but also to suffer for him...*'

'That won't go down too well, Paul, especially with those who are already saying that it's not the will of God that any Christian should be sick or suffer. They seem to think that if they're sick or suffering, then it's evident that they must have some secret sin that he's punishing them for because they won't repent.'

'God forbid, brother!'

'But James said in his letter—which was the first letter ever written to the Church—"Is any one of you sick? He should call the elders of the church to pray over him and anoint him with oil in the name of the Lord. And the prayer offered in faith will make the sick person well; the Lord will raise him up."[45] What's the matter, Paul; don't you believe in miraculous healing any more, you who have raised the dead in your ministry and healed too?'

'Epaphroditus, why did you stop your quotation there? That's not the end of James's thought. You should never treat the word of God in that way, trying to build or prove your doctrine on a sentence or two taken out of context. That will get you into all sorts of trouble. Now continue from where you stopped. Go on!'

' "If he has sinned..." '

'Say it again.'

' "If..." '

'Yes, Epaphroditus, *if*, which means that someone can be ill *without* it being directly related to a particular sin. We certainly know that ultimately all sickness is a result of the fall of man and nature into sin as a principle, but the everyday sicknesses that attack us all are not always a direct result of sin.

'Oh, I know that when Asa sinned and tried all the doctors instead of repenting, he became diseased in his feet and eventually died as a result[46] and that Nabal had a stroke and died because of sin.[47] But never forget that Elisha was persistently faithful and yet we're told that he took sick of the illness from which he died, and was even prophesying right up to the moment of his death. Yet he was as powerful in the grave as he was when he was alive.[48] His sickness was God's means of releasing him from his earthly body as his service was finished.

'I'm glad that Elisha didn't ask for a healing miracle as he approached his death, or he may have made the same mistake that Hezekiah made. Remember how he heard the word of the Lord, "This is what the Lord says: Put your house in order, because you are going to die; you will not recover." That was God's will for him. He had been the best testimony of faithfulness to God since David; the Holy Spirit-inspired programme for his life was over and it was time to go home. But what did he do? He turned his face to the wall and cried and pleaded for a miracle of healing—and got the worst thing he could ask for.'[49]

'Why do you say that, Paul?'

'Because he got fifteen more years to his life. It was during those years that he made all his mistakes and brought the nation into ruin. We're told that he didn't respond to the kindness shown him by the Lord[50] but became proud, for he considered that he'd dictated to God and that God had given in. Foolish man! God never gives in; but sometimes he does grant us his permissive will and we get what we ask for and have to live with the consequences. Oh, Epaphroditus, let's learn as believers to die on time and not hang around this ageing world and wreck the Church.'

'But, Paul, surely the Lord still heals; I mean, I heard

of a man getting his leg made longer the other day; many people saw it happen.'

'Indeed he heals, but that, my son, is not always a sign of being closer to God than those who aren't healed. After all, Jacob was a nobody with God until God shortened his leg and he limped around for the rest of his life. Don't forget that the sort of miracles to which you are referring are temporary in that they relate to our temporal world and perishable bodies; even Lazarus died again. We deal with things that are eternal, like the salvation of a soul. It has nothing to do with the length of your legs. As a matter of fact, the Lord Jesus said that, if necessary, it would be better to enter into eternal life limping, or without an eye, an arm or a foot, than to have all those and burn in the everlasting fire.'[51]

'But, Paul...'

'No "buts", my son. Remember, Stephen was a man full of the Holy Spirit. He didn't die and suffer such a death because he was not right with his Lord; he died because I helped to murder him. There's so much emphasis on healing and not enough on being saved and living a godly life. Many are willing to accept healing but not to have their personal sin-ridden souls dealt with. Even when Christ healed a whole group of lepers, only one came back to thank him, and he was a Samaritan.[52] The rest got what they wanted and took off.'

'Then if someone is sick, how will they know if it's because of some sin or not?'

'They can ask God if it's because of sin. If it is, and God is not two-faced or playing games, he will be so eager to heal and restore that one to service that, having had to use illness to get him to stop in his tracks and ask, he will respond immediately. The Spirit within that believer will pin-point and convict him of what the sin is so that he can repent. However, if he asks and God is

silent, then it was not as a result of a secret, unconfessed
sin. If someone doesn't believe that, then they are in
danger of inventing a sin so that they can have something
to repent of in the hope that the sickness will go away.
At times I get the impression that believers think that if
they're healthy, then they're spiritual people, because
underneath it all is a quest to *feel* spiritual. Some are
concentrating so hard on being "good" believers that
they forget that they're required to be good sufferers
also. Too many want to be partakers of his consoling
benefits but not his sufferings, to share in his glory but
not his pain.'[53]

'Pretty good argument, Paul, but will it convince
them?'

Paul spun round. With outstretched hands and almost
frustrated exasperation, he exclaimed, 'Write it down,
please: ... *since you are going through the same struggle you
saw I had, and now hear that I still have.* That should help to
convince them; the very experiences I have gone through
and that I'm going through right now.'

Epaphroditus did not write, but with equal appeal
said to him, 'With all due respect, Paul, that sounds like
a bunch of sour grapes to me.'

'What do you mean by that?'

'Well, just because it was a mandatory part of God's
will for your life that *you* must suffer for his name's
sake[54] doesn't mean we *all* must suffer. It will appear to
them that you're saying, "Since I suffer, then everyone
should suffer." '

'No, my son; there's a greater precedent than me for
good believing and good suffering going together—the
Lord Jesus Christ himself. I shall tell them so before I
finish this letter.'

'Right. I'll write it down. After all, in the words of
your pet phrase these days—what does it matter?'

Dear Reader

Have your religious activities changed you?

When did you last cry?

Do you agree that suffering is a part of following Christ?

Do you twist Scripture to say what you want it to say to suit your own ideas?

Do you persist in asking God for what *you* want?

Are you under the authority of his word?

Notes

41. John 17:14.
42. Acts 7:54–60.
43. Acts 9:1–17.
44. 2 Tim. 3:12.
45. James 5:14,15.
46. 2 Chron. 16:12,13.
47. 1 Sam. 25:37,38.
48. 2 Kings 13:14–21.
49. 2 Kings 20:1–6.
50. 2 Chron. 32:24,25.
51. Matt. 18:7,8.
52. Luke 17:11–17.
53. 2 Cor. 1:5–7.
54. Acts 9:15.

9

Others

Philippians 2:1–4

KJV
If there be therefore any consolation in Christ, if any comfort of love, if any fellowship of the Spirit, if any bowels and mercies.

Fulfil ye my joy, that ye be likeminded, having the same love, being of one accord, of one mind.

Let nothing be done through strife or vainglory; but in lowliness of mind let each esteem other better than themselves.

Look not every man on his own things, but every man also on the things of others.

NIV
If you have any encouragement from being united with Christ, if any comfort from his love, if any fellowship with the Spirit, if any tenderness and compassion, then make my joy complete by being like-minded, having the same love, being one in spirit and purpose. Do nothing out of selfish ambition or vain conceit, but in humility consider others better than yourselves. Each of you should look not only to your own interests, but also to the interests of others.

A T THAT LAST remark of his friend, Paul sat down wearily on the bench and leaned back against the cold wall. After a moment's staring into space, he put his elbows on his knees, cupped his head in his hands and said, 'That's one of the paradoxes of my life, Epaphroditus. In my spirit, encouraged by the Holy Spirit, I know it doesn't matter, but as far as my earthly soulishness, and in particular my feelings, are concerned, it *does* matter. I'm discovering every day that, in spite of my desire to live by faith and not feelings, my feelings are very real facts and I can still hurt.'

'Don't you know that I know that about you, Paul?'

'You know it, yes, but do you *feel* it? Do the Christians in Philippi feel it? Sometimes I think that we Christians are so caught up in our own little world, taken up with what we can "get" out of this Christianity business, that we don't even see others around us, let alone feel what others feel.

'Let's appeal to them in Philippi to feel what I'm feeling, so that instead of being critical and analytical towards my letter, they might go beyond the words and do a little feeling for me. Write this: *If you have any encouragement from being united with Christ, if any comfort from his love, if any fellowship with the Spirit, if any tenderness and compassion...* In other words: if they could find even a little capacity to give me the opposite of what they think I deserve—and after all, Epaphroditus, that's what mercy is—*then make my joy complete*—help my feelings come into line with my faith—*by being like-minded, having the same love*—that I have for them—*being one in spirit*—with me in this matter—*and purpose*—thinking with the heart for a change.'

Then, with that surprising vitality that could only be attributed to the inspiration of the Holy Spirit within him, refreshing and re-energising him, he was up on his feet again and pacing up and down, going straight into his thoughts for the benefit of the Philippian Christians. Here was a man not only appealing to them to begin to think of others for a change, but being prepared to allow the Spirit of God to distract him from the prison of his own feelings by concerning himself rather with them.

He went on: '*Do nothing out of selfish ambition or vain conceit, but in humility consider others better than yourselves.* Crazy, isn't it?'

'What's crazy, Paul?'

'Expecting human nature to do the very opposite of its natural tendency—submit and let others gain first.'

'But surely they hear enough in the preaching of the gospel, Paul, to know that they must submit to Christ?'

'I'm not talking about submission to Christ. I'm talking about the major behavioural evidence of a godly life—that of giving in and submitting to other Christians, which comes *out* of reverence for Christ.[55] Only being in a relationship with the Lord can achieve that in a person, enabling him to stand aside in favour of others.

'I mean, take Abraham for example. Look at all the trouble he got himself into because, although he was convinced of the promise of God to make his seed a great nation,[56] as the dust of the earth[57] and as the very stars in the heavens,[58] he failed on two fronts. Firstly in not leaving the bringing about of the promise in God's hands and secondly by overlooking the fact that the promise applied also to his wife. Driven by famine to Egypt and in fear of his life, he made Sarah lie about who she was, to protect his own life. When God got him out of that mess and he was back in the land, he was at once tested to see if he had learned the lesson of putting others first.'

'How was he tested, Paul?'

'Well, we're told that both he and Lot came out of Egypt loaded with livestock, silver and gold. With all that wealth, once back in the promised land their families and employees began to feel cramped and ended up fighting. Abraham was immediately aware that the

Canaanites and Perizzites were watching all this take place in the lives of those who had entered the land and claimed to be in a special relationship with the Lord. He was conscious of his need to be a testimony to them of godly behaviour.

'The natural thing for him to have done would have been to remind Lot, firstly, that he was the leader who had had the vision of God in the first place and, secondly, that he was the elder and that Lot should clear off. Abraham would have thus saved himself again and protected his own reputation before the heathen, and especially before his wife and family. However, he had learned to submit and let God do the saving. This time he allowed Lot, the younger, to choose where he wanted to live and Abraham promised he would move off in the opposite direction.'

Paul laughed.

'What's funny?'

'I've often wondered what Sarah was feeling in her tent as she listened to all this. She had a habit of eavesdropping behind the tent door.[59] I'm sure she must have felt like clapping him on the back of the head with her cooking pot and saying to him, "You stupid man, what do you think you're doing? He'll grab the best spot. What about *us*?"'

'And of course, the funny thing is that Lot did go and pick the best-watered, garden-like spot: the plain of the Jordan. But he also looked towards the city of Sodom. What an opportunity! No more desert wanderings; he and his family would be settled in a beautiful place, near a thriving city that would supply all their wants. However, the one who, with all humility, submits and lets the Almighty do the saving is in the better position. For God then told Abraham to look north, south, east and west, to go and walk through the land and enjoy it. Lot's prime, greedy, selfish spot of eternal supply was only a short time away from being wiped off the face of the earth.'[60]

They both chuckled at the wisdom of God and, while having a drink of water, discussed the awful time of pressure that Abraham must have faced from his dependants, having to contend with their feelings as well as his own until Sodom and Gomorrah were destroyed. They even wondered if anyone ever acknowledged to Abraham that, after all, he had been right to let Lot choose first. Then it was back to work.

Paul continued: '...*but in humility consider others better than yourselves. Each of you should look not only to your own interests, but also to the interests of others.* Do you know something, my friend?'

'What, Paul?'

'I was just thinking that if those wretched keys jingled right now and the guard took me out to be beheaded and asked if I had one last word for the Church, before the sword fell, without hesitation I would shout "Others!" and die happily.'

'That would be different!'

'Yes, but quite in keeping with the will of God. Did you know that Matthew mentioned that when the Lord Jesus was teaching his parables of the kingdom, he started with sowing the word of the kingdom like a seed in soil and built up to a grand climax, where one would almost expect the last parable to be about being "king of the castle", but it was the opposite? Why, the last parable he taught before he went out with dignity to face the cross was one about dividing people to the right and left and saying to those on his right, "Come, you who are blessed by my Father; take your inheritance, the kingdom prepared for you since the creation of the world." And they are going to look at him with amazement and surprise and exclaim, "Why us?", and he will say, "For I was hungry and you gave me something to eat, I was thirsty and you gave me something to drink, I was a stranger and you invited me in, I needed clothes and you clothed me, I was sick and you looked after me, I was in prison and you came to visit me." They will say to him, "When?" and his response will be, "I tell you the truth, whatever you did for one of the least of these brothers of mine, you did it for me."[61]

'Oh, Epaphroditus! If they would only learn to think about and feel for others instead of being all wrapped up in what they think they should be "getting", what a different Church and world it would be!'

'So few learn this lesson though, Paul,' said Epaphroditus thoughtfully, 'they're often too busy worshipping.'

'Worship! Now there's an area that many believers need to think more carefully about. You know earlier you mentioned the letter that James wrote? Well, have you ever noticed the definition that he gave for pure religion? He said this, "Religion that God our Father accepts as pure and faultless is this: to look after orphans and widows in their distress and to keep oneself from being polluted by the world."[62] Notice that the word he used for "religion" also means "worship"? Yes, *that* is worship; getting out and giving yourself to others and not waiting to "get" all the time. James also said there's a side-benefit from this action—you keep yourself from being polluted by the world. Christians, my son, would sin less if they were worshipping by looking after those who need to depend on others. They would be so sought after as "givers to others" that they would have no time left to sin. They would be like Stephanus of Achaia.'

'Who's he, Paul? I've never heard of him.'

'No, but if you went today to his town, walked up to

any citizen and said, "Excuse me, but can you direct me to the house of Stephanus?", without hesitation their faces would light up and they would take you there, for everyone in the town knows him. He was my first convert in that area and his family soon joined his faith. Before anyone could do a thing about it, he became an addict.'

'An addict, Paul? To what?'

'Well, he became "hooked" on serving others. He'd heard about the way Christ served and determined to follow in his steps.[63] I do pray that more and more believers will soon become addicts for this kind of worship. I long to be able to yell to the world before I leave it: "Go and get hooked on serving *others*!" '

Dear Reader

Do you still hurt?

Are you caught up in your own little world?

Have you pity and compassion for others?

Have you ever tried the ridiculous and given in to others?

Do you plan how to save yourself from problems or allow the Lord to direct you?

Are you a service 'addict'?

Notes

55. Eph. 5:21.
56. Gen. 12:2.
57. Gen. 13:16.
58. Gen. 15:5.
59. Gen. 18:10.
60. Gen. 13:1–18.
61. Matt. 25:31–46.
62. James 1:27.
63. 1 Cor. 16:15.

10

Our Prime Example

Philippians 2:5–7

KJV
Let this mind be in you, which was also in Christ Jesus:
Who, being in the form of God, thought it not robbery to be
equal with God:
But made himself no reputation, and took upon him the form
of a servant, and was made in the likeness of men...

NIV
Your attitude should be the same as that of Christ Jesus:
Who, being in very nature God,
did not consider equality with God
something to be grasped,
but made himself nothing,
taking the very nature of a servant,
being made in human likeness.

'WHAT AN UNUSUAL addiction for a man to have!'

'Not all that unusual, Epaphroditus. After all, the Lord Jesus was devoted to that end, that by what he did he might bring many sons to glory. And he achieved that through suffering.[64] So let's tell them that. Start a new paragraph: *Your attitude should be the same as that of Christ Jesus: Who, being in very nature God, did not consider equality with God something to be grasped, but made himself nothing*... Staggering, that, isn't it, brother?'

'What is, Paul?'

'That he chose to make himself nothing. Yet his Church is full of people clambering all over each other to obtain a reputation for being a good Christian, a mature leader or a saintly person. No wonder they get frustrated and have heart attacks and nervous breakdowns; they're too busy worrying about what other people think of them and trying to safeguard their reputations. There needs to be less concern over what people think about us and more taking on the attitude of Christ. Until we're able to do this, we'll frustrate the destiny God has for our lives, which is to be conformed to the likeness of his Son.[65] What really mattered to Jesus was doing the will of his Father, not what people thought of the means the Spirit revealed to him to achieve it. Take healing, for example. The method he used varied in almost every case, as did the type of person healed, the nature and cause of their affliction, their level of faith and so on. Jesus healed as directed by the Holy Spirit, according to the Father's will—not according to the traditions and expectations of men. It isn't *how* a work of God is done in a human life but *who* did it that counts, and Jesus was there to demonstrate to us who was doing it through him, namely his Father in heaven.

'Now write: ...*taking the very nature of a servant, being made in human likeness*... God became a human servant to all men when he visited this planet, this tiny speck of earth in the realms of the universe. Get that, my son; this speck of dirt, which we think is our mighty planet earth, was visited by the one who made it in the first place, and he came inside a human body, prepared in the womb of Mary to be devoted to serving. In writing that down, Epaphroditus, be sure to use the word "*doulos*".'

'But that means "slave"!'

'I know. Why, even when he was on earth he said of himself, "The Son of Man did not come to be served, but to serve."[66] Matthew used the word "*diakoneo*" to record this, which means "to serve". That's why we call those set aside in the Church to help administer it "deacons". In this sense the term means to throw away your reputation and give yourself to being the Church's slave or common labourer. Anyone who is made a deacon and doesn't become the slave of the fellowship and willing to do the commonest task is no more than a deacon that can't—how shall I say it?—"deac".'

This time they both laughed.

'Why do we always end up twisting things round?' said Epaphroditus.

'To suit ourselves and our own man-made ideas of what it means to be spiritual. We've forgotten what God has stated in his word when, in Isaiah's day, he wrote, " 'For my thoughts are not your thoughts, neither are your ways my ways,' declares the Lord. 'As the heavens are higher than the earth, so are my ways higher than your ways and my thoughts than your thoughts.' "[67] And underneath all of that is our rotten human pride that wants to be God without God's life within us. That's why I told the Roman Christians in the letter I wrote to them, "For although they knew God, they neither glorified him as God nor gave thanks to him, but their thinking became futile and their foolish hearts were darkened. Although they claimed to be wise, they became fools and exchanged the glory of the immortal God for images made to look like mortal man and birds and animals and reptiles."[68]

'Do you see the game, Epaphroditus? It's man dragging God Almighty out of the heavens and reducing him lower and lower, from God to man, then down to bird, down to animal and lower still to reptile, to a creeping thing. What creeps, my son?'

Epaphroditus looked up and with the witness of the Spirit within him, leading him gently along with Paul's inspired thoughts, he said with amazement on his face, 'A serpent—Satan!'

'Exactly. The oldest adversary in creation, whom God threw out of office in the heavens, is ever at work trying, even within the Church, to reduce God to his low level and thus make himself equal to the God who made him. It was that very Satan in his pride—which was the first sin ever committed, and that in heavenly realms, not on the earth—who once said, "I will make myself like the Most High."[69] He can never attain to God's supreme level, so works at trying to bring God down to his own level and, sad to say, his helpers are often those who claim to have the reputation of knowing God most intimately. If ever we needed Christ's example of humility in the Church, it's now.'

Dear Reader

Do you follow Christ's example?

Do you realise that the Father has predestined you to be conformed to the likeness of his Son, in *every* aspect?

Notes

64. Heb. 2:10.
65. Rom. 8:29.
66. Matt. 20:28.

67. Isa. 55:8,9.
68. Rom. 1:21–23.
69. Isa. 14:12–15.

11

Humility

Philippians 2:8–13

KJV

And being found in fashion as a man, he humbled himself, and became obedient unto death, even the death of the cross.

Wherefore God also hath highly exalted him, and given him a name which is above every name:

That at the name of Jesus every knee should bow, of things in heaven, and things in earth, and things under the earth;

And that every tongue should confess that Jesus Christ is Lord, to the glory of God the Father.

Wherefore, my beloved, as ye have always obeyed, not as in my presence only, but now much more in my absence, work out your own salvation with fear and trembling.

For it is God which worketh in you both to will and to do of his good pleasure.

NIV

And being found in appearance as a man,
he humbled himself and became obedient to death—
even death on a cross!
Therefore God exalted him to the highest place
and gave him the name that is above every name,
that at the name of Jesus every knee should bow,
in heaven and on earth and under the earth,
and every tongue confess that Jesus Christ is Lord,
to the glory of God the Father.
Therefore, my dear friends, as you have always obeyed—not

only in my presence, but now much more in my absence—
continue to work out your salvation with fear and trembling, for
it is God who works in you to will and to act according to his
good purpose.

EPAPHRODITUS STOPPED, put the pen down, went
over and sat Paul down, then fetched two cups of
water, indicating that it was time for a break.
Paul took it and they sat next to each other, legs outstretched and perched on a bench opposite them. They
drank as though they were savouring the finest of wines.
At that moment, each of them experienced the security
of being content, whatever their circumstances. Finally,
Epaphroditus broke the silence.

'I've been thinking, Paul.'

'What about?'

'How Jesus must have felt, as the Almighty God, to
be limited to a human body on the earth.'

'Probably about as excited as you'll be when you leave
your human body and find yourself like he is in eternity.
Take courage, my son; he adapted and we'll adapt to our
heavenly environment quite quickly too. However, don't
get too caught up with your imagination. You are here
and I am here and we have something yet to do or we
wouldn't be here. Now I suggest that you take your idle
body over to that table and get back to work.'

They exchanged a smile and went into action again.

'What next, Paul?'

'Let's start with the very thought you just had, friend.
Say: *And being found in appearance as a man, he humbled*
himself and became obedient to death—even death on a cross!'

'Humbled himself, Paul! But what is humility, and
shouldn't we leave God to do the humbling?'

Paul spun round quickly at those remarks.

'The answer to your first question is certainly not what
a lot of Christians think it is. You see, we all know that

pride is when you say you're the greatest, although you know in your heart of hearts that you're not. That we're all agreed on. But unfortunately some jump to the conclusion that humility is the opposite of pride; they think you have to become self-effacing and debased, declaring to everyone that you're very much worse than you are. But that's just as wrong as pride.

'No, humility is an honest assessment of what you are. In other words, if you're asked if you can—what shall I say?—sing or preach, and you know you can do neither, don't be proud and say, "Of course", or you will be asked to and you'll end up being embarrassed. But equally so, when you *can* sing or preach and are invited to do so, don't say the usual, "Oh, well, I'm not at all good at that", because that's just as big a lie and the burial of a gift. I remember explaining this to the church right here in Rome, that rather than thinking more highly of ourselves than we ought, we should think of ourselves with sober judgement, in accordance with the measure of faith God has given us for each task.'[70]

'So there is such a thing as false humility?'

'Yes, it's pride in its best disguise. And as for the second question you threw at me, never—and I repeat, *never*—ask God to humble you.'

'Why, Paul?'

'Because he might take you at face value and go ahead and do it. And you might not like the method that he will use. When the Lord has to undertake the humbling himself, it can be a painful business. Just remember what our ancestors had to go through—forty years of desert wanderings![71] We have to note that Peter agrees with me at least on that point.[72] He mentioned it to me on one occasion and in fact James also agreed.[73] We must all keep ourselves at our correct level in order that God alone will be exalted and glorified. So I repeat, although the Lord Jesus knew he was God in human flesh, he didn't go round lording it over people and pushing his superiority on them. He behaved as a very real man on this earth with a relationship to his Father in heaven, to give us a good example of humility.'

They both sat for a while in thoughtful silence.

'That's why the Lord surprised his disciples; he always did the unnatural thing. For example, John once told me that when they had all eaten together, the Twelve thought he would get up after dinner and give a speech. I mean, by that time John said they all knew who he was. John tells us that Jesus knew he came from God and would go back to God and that all power was in his hands. Can you imagine that, Epaphroditus? If you were him on that occasion, what kind of speech would you have made? But do you know what he did? He disrobed, wrapped a towel round his waist and began to wash their feet. Almighty God kneeling down washing the disciples' feet! Peter objected—and had I been there I would have done the same. Serving others was the Lord's supreme motto and he told them to do the same. He concluded by telling them that the result would be that they would be blessed.'[74]

'That's great, Paul, for I have so many asking me how to be a blessed or happy Christian. All they seem to want to hear is that in some special way the Lord by his Holy Spirit is going to do something inside them to *make* them happy. They're all looking for the secret of happiness. I wonder if they've ever tried that—being humble and serving others.'

'There's the other side to it too, Epaphroditus.'

'The other side?'

'Yes. When we humble ourselves as he humbled himself, the end result will be the same; you can go forward to *anything*, even to death on a cross, and still retain that sense of God-given happiness.

'Put this down in the letter: *Therefore God exalted him to the highest place and gave him the name that is above every name, that at the name of Jesus every knee should bow, in heaven and on earth and under the earth, and every tongue confess that Jesus Christ is Lord, to the glory of God the Father.* He will also exalt or honour us. Jesus himself said, "Whoever serves me must follow me; and where I am, my servant also will be. My Father will honour the one who serves me." '[75]

'Alas, I'm afraid, Paul, that too many want to be honoured without the service and if they serve, a service unto death is the last thing they think of.'

'Well, we have to leave them to it. Human nature, in its sinfulness, is such that some will not surrender and by choice will suffer the consequences, for at the last day all *will* so bow and confess, whether out of joy or terror at the coming of the Lord. We'd better tell them to do something about it.

'Put down further: *Therefore, my dear friends, as you have always obeyed — not only in my presence, but now much more in my absence — continue to work out your salvation with fear and trembling*... In other words, be practical in the outworking of your salvation, always afraid of your own self-efforts, and do it knowing how weak you are.'

He stopped, hand on head, trying to think, as he knew that it sounded complicated.

'Did you know, Epaphroditus, that when I was younger and was very much aware of my own utter sinfulness, despite being a church-planter, evangelist, preacher and apostle, I once said in a personal testimony "...for I have the desire to do what is good, but I cannot carry it out."[76] It was later in life that I learned to be practical to the extent that I discovered that *the Lord* was the one who worked in me to will and to do. What I could have said then is that I have the "wanting to be" a good, humble and practical Christian, but I do not have the "how to be". Now I have discovered that Christ is both my "wanting to be" and my "how to be". So put this in: *. . .for it is God who works in you to will and to act according to his good purpose.'*

'Those two thoughts together, Paul, sound great . . . "I have the wanting-to-be but don't have the how-to-be" and "Christ is both my wanting-to-be and my how-to-be". That should give them hope, for everyone who has a deep "wanting to be" must realise that it's not themselves by nature, but the Lord already at work within them, and what he has begun he will complete.'

'That's exactly what I want them to get, to know and to work out in all humility.'

'I hope they get the point!'

'So do I!'

Dear Reader

What did you think humility was?

Have you prayed for God to humble you?

Do you expect God to honour you without service?

Is he both your 'wanting to be' and 'how to be'?

Notes

70. Rom. 12:3.
71. Deut. 8:2–5.
72. 1 Peter 5:6.
73. James 4:10.

74. John 13:3–17.
75. John 12:26.
76. Rom. 7:18.

12

Lights

Philippians 2:14–18

KJV

Do all things without murmurings and disputings:

That ye may be blameless and harmless, the sons of God, without rebuke, in the midst of a crooked and perverse nation, among whom ye shine as lights in the world;

Holding forth the word of life; that I may rejoice in the day of Christ, that I have not run in vain, neither laboured in vain.

Yea, and if I be offered upon the sacrifice and service of your faith, I joy, and rejoice with you all.

For the same cause also do ye joy, and rejoice with me.

NIV

Do everything, without complaining or arguing, so that you may become blameless and pure, children of God without fault in a crooked and depraved generation, in which you shine like stars in the universe as you hold out the word of life—in order that I may boast on the day of Christ that I did not run or labour for nothing. But even if I am being poured out like a drink offering on the sacrifice and service coming from your faith, I am glad and rejoice with all of you. So you too should be glad and rejoice with me.

PAUL SCRATCHED his head and said, 'If they could only do that without making it a ground for theological argument.'

'And grumbling and murmuring when they don't win their point,' threw in Epaphroditus.

'Then put it down, for it's crucial to a good testimony that there be no fighting in front of those in darkness. Put it bluntly: *Do everything without complaining or arguing, so that you may become blameless*—no, add to that and say so that no one can find fault with your testimony for the Lord—*and pure, children of God without fault*—showing integrity and soundness of speech, and living good lives among the pagans.'[77]

'That certainly would be welcome behaviour in any church.'

'Church! Church, did you say? I'm not talking about being like that in *church*. I'm talking about being like that out there in the everyday rotten world. Put down: *...in a crooked and depraved generation...*'

'You mean, Paul, that you want believers to mix with that lot? I thought Christians were to be separate.'

'Separate for sure, but not isolated. What did Jesus pray to his Father about his disciples? He prayed, "My prayer is not that you take them out of the world but that you keep them from the evil one."[78] He wants them *in* it but not *of* it.

'That's one of the errors that are growing. Some become Christians and withdraw from the community, ending up in a new cleaner stratum of society called "church". They then try and turn it into a sort of club with their own rules for membership, the worst one being that unbelievers have to sort out their rotten sinful lives *before* they can enter a meeting. What utter nonsense! People should be attracted to the light of the gospel through believers, encouraged to come and meet God in their current condition. Then, in meeting with the Lord Jesus, they get what it takes to clean up their lives. God accepts us while we're sinners and forgives us while we're on this earth, and as we go through life in union with Christ, we should be out among the lost, helping them find the treasure that God's given to us and is longing to give to all mankind.'

'Are you hanging all that idea on one sentence of Jesus' prayer to his Father, Paul?'

'No. What did Matthew say that Jesus taught in one of his parables? He taught that his kingdom was like a man sowing good seeds—which is a picture of believers—in a field—which is the world, Epaphroditus, not a tidy, carefully tended garden. But his servants noticed that all sorts of false wheat had grown up among them. Their cry was, "Shall we go and gather them up, and do a work of separating the good from the bad right now?" And his reply was a resounding no! Rather, he said, "Let both grow together until the harvest", and the harvest was the end of the age. They are to be left growing among each other. In that way the false will at least have the opportunity to see the real and want to be like that.'[79]

'But that's impossible, Paul; a false plant can't become wheat; that would take a miracle.'

'We're dealing with just such a miracle, Epaphroditus, the miracle of rebirth. It's like ripping out a false plant-heart and putting in a wheat-heart. You can no more change an earthly sinful person into a saint than you can a false plant into wheat. They need the miracle that's even greater than a healing miracle—that of God giving someone a new birth so that they are, as it were, born again.

'If you remember, Matthew also quoted Jesus as stating, "You are the salt of the earth."[80] Salt is a preservative, it makes things tastier and slows down decomposition. That's what he wanted us to be in the world. He also said that if we've lost that purpose in society of being a deterrent to rot and no longer making life sweet and preserving it, then we're fit for nothing. He further said, "...let your light shine before men, that they may see your good deeds and praise your Father in heaven." '[81]

'That may be all very well for you, Paul; you're a big light in the kingdom. But what about those simple believers who don't feel that they're big lamps but simply sparks?'

'A spark is enough, Epaphroditus. Why, I remember walking the Ignatius Road from Neapolis to Philippi for the first time. It was night and pitch black—you couldn't see your hand in front of your face. All of a sudden I saw far off a spark, just once, and I headed for it. I soon found myself among a group sleeping by the roadside, and the spark had come from the dying embers of their fire. It was enough; I saw, I followed and I found. If every believer would be busy at their work or occupation each day but yet conscious of being a light—large or small is of no consequence—they'd be amazed at how many unbelievers would see that pin-prick of light in their darkness, come to find them and in finding them, find Christ.

'Proceed with my thoughts on that parchment, my son: ...*in which you shine like stars in the universe as you hold out the word of life—in order that I may boast on the day of Christ that I did not run or labour for nothing*. All my ministry of leading them to Christ is a sheer waste of life and time if, after coming to know him, they sit down in their worship meetings without ever getting out there to reach the lost next door, never mind the world. If they did that I would really rejoice.

'Go on: *But even if I am being poured out like a drink offering on the sacrifice and service coming from your faith, I am glad and rejoice with all of you. So you too should be glad and rejoice with me*. What I mean is, you'll be thankful that I led you out of darkness and your best way of saying thank-you for doing that is to make sure that I know, as I approach my time to die, that you're all repeating the process, out there being lights in a darkened world. Satan has unbelievers in the dark: we have to show them that there's an alternative.'

'Would you mind taking a breather, Paul, while I read that through so that I can be sure I got it all down? Besides, I need to give my wrist a rest!'

Epaphroditus quietly read through all that he had written to see if it still made sense, for when his old friend got wound up he knew that there was no stopping him. He, like Paul, could never understand anyone not caring for the lost, yet he knew full well that there was a worrying tendency among believers to neglect the vast harvest field of the world and become inward-looking and complacent.

'You finished with, "... that there is an alternative." '

'Yes, there is and they'll welcome it. The real tragedy, my son, is that those in the dark get used to living in the dark and believe that it's normal. They really believe that life is a "feeling your way through the dark". That's why I got carried away on that paragraph. We have to show them the light, for if our gospel is veiled, it's veiled to those that are lost.[82] Besides, I hate the idea of being thrown out as fit for nothing!'

Dear Reader

Are you a murmurer?

Can people find fault with you?

Are you an 'out there' Christian?

Separate or isolated?

Is your church difficult to get into?

How salty are you?

Notes

77. Titus 2:8; 1 Peter 2:12.
78. John 17:15.
79. Matt. 13:24–30,36–43.
80. Matt. 5:13.
81. Matt. 5:16.
82. 2 Cor. 4:3,4.

13

Commendation

Philippians 2:19–30

KJV

But I trust in the Lord Jesus to send Timotheus shortly unto you, that I also may be of good comfort, when I know your state.

For I have no man likeminded, who will naturally care for your state.

For all seek their own, not the things which are Jesus Christ's.

But ye know the proof of him, that, as a son with the father, he hath served with me in the gospel.

Him therefore I hope to send presently, so soon as I shall see how it will go with me.

But I trust in the Lord that I also myself shall come shortly.

Yet I supposed it necessary to send to you Epaphroditus, my brother, and companion in labour, and fellowsoldier, but your messenger, and he that ministered to my wants.

For he longed after you all, and was full of heaviness, because that ye had heard that he had been sick.

For indeed he was sick nigh unto death: but God had mercy on him; and not on him only, but on me also, lest I should have sorrow upon sorrow.

I sent him therefore the more carefully, that, when ye see him again, ye may rejoice, and that I may be the less sorrowful.

Receive him therefore in the Lord with all gladness; and hold such in reputation:

Because for the work of Christ he was nigh unto death, not regarding his life, to supply your lack of service toward me.

NIV

I hope in the Lord Jesus to send Timothy to you soon, that I also may be cheered when I receive news about you. I have no-one else like him, who takes a genuine interest in your welfare. For everyone looks out for his own interests, not those of Jesus Christ. But you know that Timothy has proved himself, because as a son with his father he has served with me in the work of the gospel. I hope, therefore, to send him as soon as I see how things go with me. And I am confident in the Lord that I myself will come soon.

But I think it is necessary to send back to you Epaphroditus, my brother, fellow-worker and fellow-soldier, who is also your messenger, whom you sent to take care of my needs. For he longs for all of you and is distressed because you heard he was ill. Indeed he was ill, and almost died. But God had mercy on him, and not on him only but also on me, to spare me sorrow upon sorrow. Therefore I am all the more eager to send him, so that when you see him again you may be glad and I may have less anxiety. Welcome him in the Lord with great joy, and honour men like him, because he almost died for the work of Christ, risking his life to make up for the help you could not give me.

'I KNOW I'm approaching my time to die, Epaphroditus, but I really am able to rejoice, you know. I've just thought of another reason why it doesn't matter if I get out of here or not. Even if they do cut my head off and think that in so doing they'll silence the gospel, what amuses me is that I have helped to prepare many other voices to take over for me. For every voice that they stop, our work as pastors is to get another few ready to replace those stopped ones. I think particularly of Timothy. I'm so happy that I got him ready. I believe I'll drop him a line and send him to your church. So say this...'

Epaphroditus dipped the pen in his ink-pot again and poised it over the parchment, ready to begin.

'*I hope in the Lord Jesus to send Timothy to you soon...*
Mind you, we need to be careful about whom we send,
Epaphroditus. We usually choose the most likely, best
equipped and best educated person, whom we feel is just
right. However, the Almighty knows best. Who would
ever have imagined that revival and freedom for Israel
from under the Moabites would take place when God
sent a left-handed, temperamental misfit like Ehud to be
the deliverer. I told you about my Benjamite ancestor
earlier, didn't I, when we were discussing my temperament? Anyway, a committee wouldn't have even considered him on a short list, yet in God's wisdom he was
created just for that time, place and purpose. He was
appointed an ambassador and was sent with tribute to
King Eglon of Moab. But Ehud had strapped a sword to
his right thigh and with his left hand took it out and
struck Eglon down.'[83]

'I never really thought much about the character of
the people the Lord choses to do his will, but now I see
what you mean, Paul,' said Epaphroditus: 'Moses an ex-
murderer, Samson an adulterer, David a shepherd.'

'And don't forget that even Jael with a hammer and a
tent-peg was sent by God to win a battle and turn the
tide of history,'[84] Paul reminded him.

'Is that what you meant when you once said that the
foolishness of God is wiser than men's wisdom?'[85]

'Quite. So continue: ...*that I also may be cheered when I
receive news about you. I have no-one else like him, who takes a
genuine interest in your welfare.* It's a good feeling to be able
to tell them that of all the pastors I've prepared, there's
no one with whom I can compare Timothy for dedication, and I can commend him thoroughly.'

'I wonder how many pastors out there, Paul, can look
at their fellowships today, and at short notice choose a

committed person to step in to replace them. Why are there so few?'

'My next sentence in the letter is the answer you seek, friend: *For everyone looks out for his own interests, not those of Jesus Christ.* It's basically selfishness we're talking about . . . *But you know that Timothy has proved himself, because as a son with his father he has served with me in the work of the gospel. I hope, therefore, to send him as soon as I see how things go with me. And I am confident in the Lord that I myself will come soon. But I think it is necessary to send back to you Epaphroditus . . .*'

At this, Epaphroditus threw down his pen and jumped to his feet, an expression of amazement on his face.

'And when did you think *that*, might I ask? You've never discussed it with me. What gave you the idea that I would leave you? Who would look after you if I were not here?'

Paul smiled at his bristling companion. 'It's time you had a break from all this. Although you're not a prisoner, you've made yourself one by coming in here day after day throughout my being in prison, to labour for me and wash my clothes and prepare my food. Timothy is not the only one I can commend for his dedication, so calm down and keep writing.'

That seemed to take him aback and he sat down, mouth opened in disbelief.

'Me? Rank with Timothy? Impossible! What have I done but those everyday chores that were necessary to help you in your present plight? I mean, I can't preach like Timothy, nor am I a gifted pastor. I can only wash clothes and dishes, empty your toilet bucket and write your letters.'

'Who knows, my son, maybe one day something you

write with that pen of yours could be copied and read by many people.'

'Nonsense!'

'Be that as it may, write these words for me now: ...*my brother, fellow-worker and fellow-soldier*... Yes, you are all that to me. Your very breathing in this room is a gift. Epaphroditus, thank you for being beside me every time I allowed myself to feel depressed. That has meant more to me than anything else and I shall tell your church so. Write down: ...*who is also your messenger, whom you sent to take care of my needs.*

'Actually, you always went beyond my needs to give me some wants too—things that I could have managed without but you always went further in your love for me. I've deeply appreciated that, and I love you too, friend. They sent you here to deliver gifts to help me, and you ended up staying. They probably thought for a while that you'd been living it up in the big city. But now they're worried about you because they've heard that you were very ill for a while. I want to tell them about that illness.'

'No! Please, I don't want them to know about that.'

'It's my letter, so write or I'll write it myself.'

'Very well, if you insist.'

'I do, so say: *For he longs for all of you and is distressed because you heard he was ill. Indeed he was ill, and almost died. But God had mercy on him, and not on him only but also on me, to spare me sorrow upon sorrow.* You see, my son, you have been the means of keeping me going with your steadfast courage. I know I'm not the easiest person to work for. How you managed through all my stubbornness and awkwardness and my own ill health I'll never know—the way you drove yourself until it made you ill. I was so busy receiving from you that I fear I ended up taking you for granted and was blind to the fact that it was making you ill. You must forgive me for that.'

'There's nothing to forgive, Paul. I was happy to do it. In fact, my having the desire and opportunity to help you in this way may, I believe, have made the church realise that you were being neglected.'

'H'm. Well, put down next: *Therefore I am all the more eager to send him, so that when you see him again you may be glad and I may have less anxiety. Welcome him in the Lord with great joy, and honour men like him, because he almost died for the work of Christ, risking his life to make up for the help you could not give me.*'

'Paul, *must* you put that in? I'd rather you didn't.'

'Leave it in. It will help remind them that a person can be so committed to Christ and serving him, selflessly, as you have, that he can end up nearly working himself to death. I want to emphasise, too, that your illness wasn't because of some secret sin but because you were wearing yourself out for the work of Christ. Had I not been so blind I would have stopped you sooner and made you take a rest.

'Why, even the Lord made his disciples go apart for a while and have a break because he saw that their enthusiasm was such that they would have become worn out serving him.[86] And don't forget that the Lord himself sat on a well's mouth in Samaria, weary. Yes, if the Almighty in a physical body could be tired, who are we to think that we should have boundless energy twenty-four hours a day and should never show a bit of tiredness? It's stupid, Epaphroditus. And some are even suggesting that it's a glorious thing to "burn out for God", whether or not he particularly wants it. I have a feeling that he is eager to do so much more through his children but is often hindered because they have a "self-burn-out" and are finished before he intended. Oh, may we find the humility and grace to live inside our limits and remember that we are but dust.'

'But, Paul! Did he not say that *without* him we could do nothing?[87] Then surely that means that *with* him we can do anything?'

'Logically, yes. But it may well be that he might not want to do *everything* through you or me. That's what I'm learning here in prison. I kept the work to myself for too long. Now I'm seeing that he wants to share it round and do it through the entire body of Christ, which is made up of many members. You and I are not the entire body, friend, but simply a part of it. That's why I'm sending you away, to go back home. I want you to remember me for what you knew and saw, and for our great times of fellowship together. I don't want you here when they finally decide to take my life. I want your last vision to be of us together, alive. Please make me happy in this by going home soon.'

'You may be right, although I feel I should stay longer. But I will go, if it'll make you happy.'

'Good, for I want to commend you to God and to your church, and remember, I don't want you arriving in Philippi burnt out.'

Dear Reader

Are you commendable?

Whose interests do you seek?

Are you a companion to believers?

How much do you expect Christ to do through you?

Are you running races that God did not intend for you?

Notes

83. Judg. 3:16–22.
84. Judg. 4:17–22.
85. 1 Cor. 1:25.
86. Mark 6:31.
87. John 15:5.

14

Beware!

Philippians 3:1—4:1

KJV

Finally, my brethren, rejoice in the Lord. To write the same things to you, to me indeed is not grievous, but for you it is safe.

Beware of dogs, beware of evil workers, beware of the concision.

For we are the circumcision, which worship God in the spirit, and rejoice in Christ Jesus, and have no confidence in the flesh.

Though I might also have confidence in the flesh. If any other man thinketh that he hath whereof he might trust in the flesh, I more:

Circumcised the eighth day, of the stock of Israel, of the tribe of Benjamin, an Hebrew of the Hebrews; as touching the law, a Pharisee;

Concerning zeal, persecuting the church; touching the righteousness which is in the law, blameless.

But what things were gain to me, those I counted loss for Christ.

Yea doubtless, and I count all things but loss for the excellency of the knowledge of Christ Jesus my Lord: for whom I have suffered the loss of all things, and do count them but dung, that I may win Christ,

And be found in him, not having mine own righteousness, which is of the law, but that which is through the faith of Christ, the righteousness which is of God by faith:

That I may know him, and the power of his resurrection, and the fellowship of his sufferings, being made conformable unto his death;

If by any means I might attain unto the resurrection of the dead.

Not as though I had already attained, either were already perfect: but I follow after, if that I may apprehend that for which also I am apprehended of Christ Jesus.

Brethren, I count not myself to have apprehended: but this one thing I do, forgetting those things which are behind, and reaching forth unto those things which are before,

I press toward the mark for the prize of the high calling of God in Christ Jesus.

Let us therefore, as many as be perfect, be thus minded: and if in any thing ye be otherwise minded, God shall reveal even this unto you.

Nevertheless, whereto we have already attained, let us walk by the same rule, let us mind the same thing.

Brethren, be followers together of me, and mark them which walk so as ye have us for an ensample.

(For many walk, of whom I have told you often, and now tell you even weeping, that they are the enemies of the cross of Christ:

Whose end is destruction, whose God is their belly, and whose glory is in their shame, who mind earthly things.)

For our conversation is in heaven; from whence also we look for the Saviour, the Lord Jesus Christ:

Who shall change our vile body, that it may be fashioned like unto his glorious body, according to the working whereby he is able even to subdue all things unto himself.

Therefore, my brethren dearly beloved and longed for, my joy and crown, so stand fast in the Lord, my dearly beloved.

NIV

Finally, my brothers, rejoice in the Lord! It is no trouble for me to write the same things to you again, and it is a safeguard for you.

Watch out for those dogs, those men who do evil, those mutilators of the flesh. For it is we who are the circumcision, we who worship by the Spirit of God, who glory in Christ Jesus, and who put no confidence in the flesh—though I myself have reasons for such confidence.

If anyone else thinks he has reasons to put confidence in the flesh, I have more: circumcised on the eighth day, of the people of Israel, of the tribe of Benjamin, a Hebrew of Hebrews; in regard to the law, a Pharisee; as for zeal, persecuting the church; as for legalistic righteousness, faultless.

But whatever was to my profit I now consider loss for the sake of Christ. What is more, I consider everything a loss compared to the surpassing greatness of knowing Christ Jesus my Lord, for whose sake I have lost all things. I consider them rubbish, that I may gain Christ and be found in him, not having a righteousness of my own that comes from the law, but that which is through faith in Christ—the righteousness that comes from God and is by faith. I want to know Christ and the power of his resurrection and the fellowship of sharing in his sufferings, becoming like him in his death, and so, somehow, to attain to the resurrection from the dead.

Not that I have already obtained all this, or have already been made perfect, but I press on to take hold of that for which Christ Jesus took hold of me. Brothers, I do not consider myself yet to have taken hold of it. But one thing I do: Forgetting what is behind and straining towards what is ahead, I press on towards the goal to win the prize for which God has called me heavenwards in Christ Jesus.

All of us who are mature should take such a view of things. And if on some point you think differently, that too God will make clear to you. Only let us live up to what we have already attained.

Join with others in following my example, brothers, and take note of those who live according to the pattern we gave you. For, as I have often told you before and now say again even with tears, many live as enemies of the cross of Christ. Their destiny is destruction, their god is their stomach, and their glory is in their shame. Their mind is on earthly things. But our citizenship is in heaven. And we eagerly await a Saviour from there, the Lord Jesus Christ, who, by the power that enables him to bring everything under his control, will transform our lowly bodies so that they will be like his glorious body.

Therefore, my brothers, you whom I love and long for, my joy and crown, that is how you should stand firm in the Lord, dear friends!

THE SHADOWS lengthened as the sun sank low in the western sky. Epaphroditus peered at the parchment with some difficulty. He stopped writing and, knowing that night and day were getting more and more alike to Paul with his bad eyesight, remarked, 'It's getting late. We've not so much as stopped for our evening meal yet and my nose is getting very near the ink-pot. How about stopping until the morning?'

'Can you guarantee me the morning, Epaphroditus?'

He did not reply but, standing up, pulled the table nearer the little window. Re-positioning his chair, he now sat with his back to the apostle, waiting for what was to be written next.

'Thank you, my friend. I don't have a lot more to say and you're right; it's getting late. Besides, I could go on and on with what I want to tell them, so let's try and draw it to a close.'

He paced up and down for a while before beginning again: '*Finally, my brothers, rejoice in the Lord! It is no trouble for me to write the same things to you again, and it is a safeguard for you.* I mean, I know you so well that I can trust you with these thoughts, knowing that you're mature enough to take them without misinterpreting them. *Watch out for those dogs, those men who do evil, those mutilators of the flesh.*'

'You've never been able to forget what those legalistic Judaistic religionists did to your converts and young churches years ago, have you, Paul?'

'No. It was so devastating, especially since I'd come out of all that mess myself. It really hurt to see young Christians being lured back under law. Ezekiel's prophetic words against false shepherds still apply today. He said that their main errors were looking after themselves and their own self-righteous positions of authority and failing to care for the weak and sick. Force and cruelty had ruled over the flock until many left and became scattered without any shepherds to care for them.[88] I'm just so afraid that it will happen all over again when I'm gone.'

'The Lord is quite able to take care of that problem, Paul.'

'True, but that won't stop those legalists from trying to bring Christians under their tyrannical systems. They'll go on trying to add to God's revealed means of achieving righteousness—faith in Jesus Christ.[89] But that way is all empty. I tried it for years.'

'Then why don't you give them your testimony, Paul? It might help.'

'All right, put this down: *For it is we who are the circumcision, we who worship by the Spirit of God, who glory in Christ Jesus, and who put no confidence in the flesh*—or self-effort—*though I myself have reasons for such confidence. If anyone else thinks he has reasons to put confidence in the flesh, I have more: circumcised on the eighth day, of the people of Israel, of the tribe of Benjamin, a Hebrew of Hebrews; in regard to the law, a Pharisee...* Just think of that, Epaphroditus. As far as reputation was concerned, I was known as one who was most zealous for the traditions of my fathers. Nor was I content having received that accolade; I worked very hard to keep it—yes, to keep my reputation—by persecuting the Church of God.[90]

'Continue: *...as for zeal*'—and with tears running down his face, overcome with the memory of it all, he barely whispered the next phrase—'*persecuting the church; as for legalistic righteousness, faultless. But whatever was to my profit I now consider loss for the sake of Christ. What is more, I consider everything a loss compared to the surpassing greatness of* *knowing Christ Jesus my Lord... My* Lord, Epaphroditus. It's a staggering thought that I could haul Christians to jail and even death, and be such a blasphemer, and yet the Lord had such mercy on me that I'm allowed to call him *my* Lord; *...for whose sake I have lost all things. I consider them rubbish, that I may gain Christ and be found in him, not having a righteousness of my own that comes from the law, but that which is through faith in Christ—the righteousness that comes from God and is by faith.*

'Yes, *that* is the goal; if I could only get everyone to see it! It isn't being a stalwart of the faith, or even simply a Christian; not following this or that set of rules, or believing this or that, but gaining the very *person* of Christ. I've come to realise that my theological viewpoint was nothing more or less than rubbish—I'd go so far as to say dung—compared with what I found when I stepped by God's grace into that intimate relationship of knowing him personally.'

'It took me a long time to see that also, Paul,' said Epaphroditus. 'How I often wish we could make all Christians instantly see it, say by preaching a sermon that would explain it so clearly that they would all want Christ more than anything else.'

'That's the amazing thing, Epaphroditus. *We* can't make that happen, however powerful our words. Believers just need to concentrate on *knowing* him; if only they realised that it's not me, Paul, who is powerful, nor has that ever been my goal. Write: *I want to know Christ and the power of his resurrection and the fellowship of sharing in his sufferings, becoming like him in his death, and so, somehow, to attain to the resurrection from the dead. Not that I have already obtained all this, or have already been made perfect, but I press on to take hold of that for which Christ Jesus took hold of me.*'

'It's strange to hear you talk like that, Paul. Most of us

who have known you for years and watched you closely often wish we had your maturity. We keep thinking in terms of catching up with you and here you are blowing away that image by saying that even you have further to go.'

'Then that should give other believers hope. Once they become aware that I've been able to break away from all that self-righteous religion and have been used by God to lead others to Christ, form fellowships and build up the flock—while still being far from perfection—they'll see that the Lord can do it through them also.

'This idea of needing to reach maturity in order to be used by God is one of the enemy's greatest tricks. Concentrating on becoming spiritual enough is the opposite of what we need, because we'll always be convinced that we're not mature enough. That's why we have to come through to knowing Christ, for it is *he* who will do it, through our weakness. Say: *Brothers, I do not consider myself yet to have taken hold of it. But one thing I do: Forgetting what is behind and straining towards what is ahead, I press on towards the goal to win the prize for which God has called me heavenwards in Christ Jesus.'*

'That's great, Paul—forgetting things behind and reaching to things ahead. I'm amazed at how big an enemy my own memory has been in my life and how it's prevented me from going on with God.'

'Yes, we should beware of dwelling on the past. It's too easy to day-dream and go back into our memories to imagine how it could have been had we gone down a road other than the one we did go down. But that's a waste of time. We were never built to carry yesterday on our backs as well as today; that will only break us and prevent us from letting God use us as he wants to. God has forgiven and forgotten the past; we need to do the same.[91]

'But a greater thing to beware of, Epaphroditus, is trying to carry tomorrow on our backs as well. That's the enemy's subtlety; he either gets us enmeshed in the past or worrying about the future. No, we are to press on to what is in front of us now and do what we can now. That's why I asked you earlier if you could give me tomorrow. We must learn to live in the present tense of things.'

'Are you saying that we should never plan for tomorrow, Paul?'

'Not at all. Part of my today may be saying yes to a programme or plan for the future, but I put it all in the Lord's hands, leaving it to him to encourage, block or redirect. Once we're really able to place our lives in his hands and accept that he is concerned with our ultimate good, we see that such occurrences are simply his adjusting circumstances to achieve that good.

'Too many have missed this. Some sit and wait for an architectural drawing of their entire future before they'll move out and do anything, and because no plan arrives in a letter from heaven, they never move. Then there are those who get a vision for tomorrow and run out and try to do it all today. That's just as crazy. Joseph did that. His vision was clear: he was to be a means of salvation to his family. He ran from the presence of God to gather the family to tell them and it all collapsed round him.[92] It was twenty years later that he was able to see that the vision was right; it was his timing that was wrong.'[93]

He paused and laughed a little, then went on: 'I did that myself, right after I was converted. Ananias told me that the Lord had told him his will for my life—that I was to be his alone and set aside to carry his name before the Gentiles and their kings, and before the people of

Israel, and to suffer. I ran out to do it all as soon as I could. How humiliating it all looked when the fellowship found me too hot to handle, stuck me in a basket and let me down over the wall! As I ran from there to Arabia, I wondered what had gone wrong and why I had been so let down. Huh! An apostle in a basket!

'But looking back now, I can see that I was getting it all wrong. The Lord said Gentiles, their kings and Israel—but I started with Israel. He adjusted things to make me head for the Gentiles. The kings and the suffering I have experienced, but alas, I feel that I haven't fulfilled the last part yet—reaching Israel. They didn't want me or my message, but I so long for their conversion that I'd count myself accursed just to see one of them converted.'[94]

He then began to speak steadily and quietly, his voice betraying a sense of shame as he went on. 'Did you know that when I realised a few years ago that I was running out of health and time, I decided to take myself back to Jerusalem and get the job done before it was too late? Although I felt compelled by the Spirit, the amazing thing was that in every city I went through, the Holy Spirit warned me that prison and hardships were facing me.[95] Even when I reached as near as Tyre, I was warned again by the Holy Spirit through the disciples there, who urged me not to go on to Jerusalem.[96] Do you know what I did?'

'No! What?'

'I dug my heels in and went on. When I got to Caesarea, we went to stay with Philip and while we were there Agabus came in from Jerusalem. I had never met him before nor he me. He was placing his cloak with the others in the entrance way when he suddenly picked up my belt, tied himself up with it and prophesied in the power of the Holy Spirit that the man who owned that belt would be bound in like manner and handed over to the Gentiles.'[97]

'Did you still go on?'

'Of course I did. You know me; stubborn to the end, even after the warning of the Holy Spirit. So, in due course, I was arrested in Jerusalem and the events took place that brought me to where I am now. I don't know if I'll ever get back that part of my programme to reach Israel. Maybe I've forfeited that part through disobedience.'

He wept quietly again and Epaphroditus went over and sat with his arm around his shoulders for a while. He advised Paul gently that he should listen to his own preaching right now, forget the past and press on. He also reminded him of their earlier conversation when Paul himself had pointed out that while the Lord supplies the strength to do all that he has commanded, he might not want to achieve everything through one person. It was not the Lord's intention that Paul alone convert the whole nation of Israel, and in testifying to the Jews that Jesus was the Christ, at every opportunity, he had in fact fulfilled his commission to carry Jesus' name before the people of Israel.[98]

As Paul regained his composure, Epaphroditus got to his feet again, returned to his chair at the table and picked up the pen, as his dear friend prepared to continue.

'*All of us who are mature should take such a view of things. And if on some point you think differently, that too God will make clear to you. Only let us live up to what we have already attained. Join with others in following my example, brothers, and take note of those who live according to the pattern we gave you. For, as I have often told you before and now say again even with tears, many live as enemies of the cross of Christ. Their destiny is destruction, their god is their stomach, and their glory is in their*

shame. *Their mind is on earthly things*. Oh, that they would beware of earthly things.'

At this he turned round and asked his friend a question.

'Epaphroditus, why did God destroy Sodom and Gomorrah?'

'What a strange question, Paul. Why, because they were sexually impure—everyone knows that.'

'Yes, I know that's the usually accepted reason, but it's not the worst thing they did; that behaviour was the outcome of what had happened before.'

'Where did you get that from, Paul?'

'From Ezekiel, who wrote that Sodom's sins were first arrogance, then overfeeding and total unconcern for and disregard of the poor and needy.[99] Such selfishness gave them all the time they needed for their abominations. That's one of the reasons why it's dangerous to equate health, wealth and prosperity with being spiritual; it could be the prelude to abominable behaviour. So conclude my paragraph with these closing remarks: *But our citizenship is in*—and we should therefore exhibit behaviour suited to—*heaven. And we eagerly await a Saviour from there, the Lord Jesus Christ, who, by the power that enables him to bring everything under his control, will transform our lowly bodies so that they will be like his glorious body. Therefore, my brothers, you whom I love and long for, my joy and crown, that is how you should stand firm in the Lord, dear friends!* I have warned you. Beware.'

Dear Reader

Are you a shepherd?

What kind?

Do you demonstrate your power or Christ's?

Do you think you have arrived?

Have you dreams and hopes and visions?

Do you try to implement them or wait for the Lord's timing?

Are you aware of the subtlety of the sin of Sodom?

Notes

88. Ezek. 34:1–15.
89. Gal. 2:16; Rom. 10:4.
90. Gal. 1:13,14.
91. Jer. 31:33,34.
92. Gen. 37:1–28.
93. Gen. 45:1–8.
94. Rom. 9:1–3; 10:1.
95. Acts 20:23.
96. Acts 21:4.
97. Acts 21:10,11.
98. Acts 9:15.
99. Ezek. 16:49,50.

15

Women?

Philippians 4:2,3

KJV

I beseech Euodias, and beseech Syntyche, that they be of the same mind in the Lord.

And I intreat thee also, true yokefellow, help those women which laboured with me in the gospel, with Clement also, and with other my fellowlabourers, whose names are in the book of life.

NIV

I plead with Euodia and I plead with Syntyche to agree with each other in the Lord. Yes, and I ask you, loyal yoke-fellow, help these women who have contended at my side in the cause of the gospel, along with Clement and the rest of my fellow-workers, whose names are in the book of life.

EPAPHRODITUS LOOKED up from the scratchings of his pen: 'Do you really think that one letter can bring all the Philippian believers into standing fast in the Lord with one heart and spirit, Paul?'

'Why, don't you think it will be a means of bringing them together that way?'

'The majority, yes; but I'm thinking of two of our women who always seem to be at loggerheads!'

'You don't mean Euodia and Syntyche? I thought we'd straightened all that out.'

'It lasted a week or two, then went back to what has become the norm. In fact, behind their backs the people have nicknamed them "Odious" and "Soon-touchy"!'

'Then let's try once more. Put down: *I plead with Euodia and I plead with Syntyche to agree with each other in the Lord. Yes, and I ask you, loyal yoke-fellow*...'

'Which yoke-fellow, Paul?'

'He'll know who I mean. Just write it as I dictate it.'

'Why can't you name him? I mean, shouldn't we be fair? After all, you mentioned Timothy by name. If you mention one servant of the Lord, why not make it a rule to mention them all?'

'The Lord himself didn't always mention names. We know the names of the twelve apostles, but don't forget that he sent out seventy-two others also.[100] The need for recognition is of no consequence to mature believers because they know that without the Lord they can do nothing. They'll be thanking him and giving him the credit for whatever he accomplishes through them, for it is *him* doing it. Don't forget what Jesus said when on earth: "Be careful not to do your 'acts of righteousness' before men, to be seen by them. If you do, you will have no reward from your Father in heaven." '[101]

'All right, I'll put down what you say, but I'm still not certain about that one.'

'So we shall go on: ...*loyal yoke-fellow, help these women who have contended at my side in the cause of the gospel*...'

'You know, Paul, it seems strange that you had women on your outreach team. I thought you advocated to some of the churches that women should be seen and not heard in church.'

'When did I say that, Epaphroditus?'

'Well, to the Corinthian church, for one. Let me think how you said it...'

'I know exactly how I said it, young man.[102] I said that

women should keep silent in church, but let me explain what I meant. You seem to be rather confused.

'Now, you know that it's been the custom for women not to be allowed to be part of the worship. This is largely being carried out in the church by the fathers and sons, just as it is in the synagogues. In the Jewish tradition, mothers and daughters have always been considered to be incapable of learning at any level. In worship they're prevented from participating, and relegated to standing behind a lattice-work screen or upstairs. Naturally enough, having been excluded from the proceedings, all they do is chatter to each other about who's getting married, where they get their dress material and who's having babies. It concerns me that this attitude is widespread in the church as well. In my letter to the Corinthian church, I wasn't demeaning women; I was exhorting them, raising them to their God-given equality with men. I was, in effect, telling them to come out from behind the screen, sit down, stop chattering and start using the brains that they've been given to learn, along with the men. After all, in Christ Jesus there is neither male nor female, but we are all one in him.[103]

'Remember also that the fellowships have the habit of sitting in a segregated fashion, women on one side and men on the other. Can you imagine the chaos of noise that would take place if a speaker were teaching and some of the women had a question on what had just been said and started shouting across the room at their men for an explanation? That's why I asked them to wait until they got home.'

'Didn't you also tell Timothy not to let a woman teach in the church?'

'No, again that's being misunderstood. I was once more encouraging women to learn. My remarks were about not "usurping" authority over male teachers, being just beginners in studying God's word, and a caution to remember that it was Eve who was deceived.[104] I also warned Timothy that when a false teacher enters a district, he tends to head straight for the uneducated women in the church to perpetrate his pernicious lies.[105]

'So, when I had women helpers in my team, they didn't push their way in, nor did they run around getting others to convince me to let them help. I was in no way usurped; I delegated the tasks to them. Remember that I also referred to women praying and prophesying in my letter to the Corinthians.'[106]

'So it's all right for women to speak God's word?'

'Well, Epaphroditus, where would the gospel of Christ, or even his coming into the world, be if it had not been for God using the likes of Rahab the prostitute[107] and Ruth the Moabitess,[108] both of whom are in the direct line of ascent from Adam to Christ?[109] Thank God for Israel's victory through Jael with her hammer and tent-peg, when she slew Sisera. And don't forget the prophetess Deborah who was leading Israel at that time.[110] David again and again submitted to the wisdom of women and prevented himself from causing some pretty big disasters: Abigail;[111] the wise woman of Tekoah;[112] the wise woman of Abel;[113] and Bathsheba.[114]

'Why, where would we be today without Mary offering herself to be the vessel through whom the power of the Almighty descended to conceive in her the human body in which the very Christ of God was to live for thirty-three years?[115] I doubt very much if a leading priest would have been able to achieve that! Why, even when Mary took Jesus to be circumcised, it was Anna the prophetess who declared him to be who he was to those who looked forward to the redemption of Jerusalem.[116] Then again, don't forget that the first to declare him risen from the dead to a bunch of scared men locked in an upper room were the women,[117] and later Christ appeared and rebuked the men for not believing their word.[118] In fact, Mary Magdalene could be described as the first apostle or "sent one", commissioned directly by the risen Lord.[119]

'Go on into the very early days of the Church and you'll find Dorcas;[120] my first Macedonian convert was Lydia—she looked after me well;[121] then, of course, there was Priscilla;[122] and the four prophesying daughters of Philip the evangelist...'[123]

'Prophesying, Paul; isn't that foretelling the future as directed by the Holy Spirit?'

'It certainly can be, but not necessarily. When Moses was digging in his heels and complaining that he wasn't a good speaker, the Almighty said to him, "What about your brother, Aaron the Levite? I know he can speak well.... You shall speak to him and put words in his mouth; I will help both of you speak and will teach you what to do. He will speak to the people for you, and it will be as if he were your mouth and as if you were God to him."[124]

'Later, when Moses was again trying to excuse himself before the Lord: "Then the Lord said to Moses, 'See, I have made you like God to Pharaoh, and your brother Aaron will be your prophet.'[125] Well, Epaphroditus, if you follow all the things that the Lord said to Moses, Moses said to Aaron and Aaron said to Pharaoh, you'll have to note that it wasn't always referring to the future. Prophecy can be about the past and present as well as the future. Basically, when people prophesy they are speaking for God under the anointing of the Holy Spirit. This can take two forms: the forth-telling, which I've just explained and which includes preaching, teaching and evangelism; and foretelling future events. Whatever form it takes, the gift of prophecy is for building up the church.[126] Though not everyone has the ministry of prophet,[127] all can prophesy,[128] as indeed prophesied by Joel![129] Does that make it clearer?"

'Well, I'll have to think some more about it. Meanwhile, proceed with what you were dictating. You left off at: "... these women who have contended at my side in the cause of the gospel".'

'*...along with Clement and the rest of my fellow-workers, whose names are in the book of life.* That's the important thing, Epaphroditus; not whether they get mentioned by name or whether they're men or women, but that their names are in the Lamb's book of life. That's more than any reputation and, as far as I'm concerned, knowing that I might never get out to preach again, I'll be glad of any voice that will declare the Lord Jesus Christ, whether male or female, and, as we are getting used to saying to each other today, what does it matter? After all, some men I've heard preach have nothing to say, even after a lifetime of study and experience!'

Dear Reader

Are you upset if you do not get mentioned?

Have you really studied women in Scripture?

Do you agree with Scripture's declaration of prophecy?

Notes

100. Luke 10:1.
101. Matt. 6:1.
102. 1 Cor. 14:34,35.
103. Gal. 3:28.
104. 1 Tim. 2:11,12,14.
105. 2 Tim. 3:1–7.
106. 1 Cor. 11:5.
107. Josh. 2:1–13; Heb. 11:31.
108. Ruth 1:4.
109. Matt. 1:5.
110. Judg. 4:1–24.
111. 1 Sam. 25:18–31.
112. 2 Sam. 14:4–22.
113. 2 Sam. 20:14–22.
114. 1 Kings 1:15.
115. Luke 1:26–38.
116. Luke 2:36–38.
117. Luke 24:5–11.
118. Mark 16:14.
119. John 20:17,18.
120. Acts 9:36.
121. Acts 16:14.
122. Acts 18.
123. Acts 21:9.
124. Exod. 4:14–16.
125. Exod. 7:1.
126. 1 Cor. 14:3.
127. Eph. 4:11.
128. 1 Cor. 14:31.
129. Joel 2:28.

16

Joy and Generosity

Philippians 4:4–23

KJV
Rejoice in the Lord alway: and again I say, Rejoice.

Let your moderation be known unto all men. The Lord is at hand.

Be careful for nothing; but in every thing by prayer and supplication with thanksgiving let your requests be made known unto God.

And the peace of God, which passeth all understanding, shall keep your hearts and minds through Christ Jesus.

Finally, brethren, whatsoever things are true, whatsoever things are honest, whatsoever things are just, whatsoever things are pure, whatsoever things are lovely, whatsoever things are of good report; if there be any virtue, and if there be any praise, think on these things.

Those things, which ye have both learned, and received, and heard, and seen in me, do: and the God of peace shall be with you.

But I rejoiced in the Lord greatly, that now at the last your care of me hath flourished again; wherein ye were also careful, but ye lacked opportunity.

Not that I speak in respect of want: for I have learned, in whatsoever state I am, therewith to be content.

I know both how to be abased, and I know how to abound: every where and in all things I am instructed both to be full and to be hungry, both to abound and to suffer need.

I can do all things through Christ which strengtheneth me.

Notwithstanding ye have well done, that ye did communicate with my affliction.

Now ye Philippians know also, that in the beginning of the gospel, when I departed from Macedonia, no church communicated with me as concerning giving and receiving, but ye only.

For even in Thessalonica ye sent once and again unto my necessity.

Not because I desire a gift: but I desire fruit that may abound to your account.

But I have all, and abound: I am full, having received of Epaphroditus the things which were sent from you, an odour of a sweet smell, a sacrifice acceptable, wellpleasing to God.

But my God shall supply all your need according to his riches in glory by Christ Jesus.

Now unto God and our Father be glory for ever and ever. Amen.

Salute every saint in Christ Jesus. The brethren which are with me greet you.

All the saints salute you, chiefly they that are of Caesar's household.

The grace of our Lord Jesus Christ be with you all. Amen.

NIV

Rejoice in the Lord always. I will say it again: Rejoice! Let your gentleness be evident to all. The Lord is near. Do not be anxious about anything, but in everything, by prayer and petition, with thanksgiving, present your requests to God. And the peace of God, which transcends all understanding, will guard your hearts and your minds in Christ Jesus.

Finally, brothers, whatever is true, whatever is noble, whatever is right, whatever is pure, whatever is lovely, whatever is admirable—if anything is excellent or praiseworthy—think about such things. Whatever you have learned or received or heard from me, or seen in me—put it into practice. And the God of peace will be with you.

I rejoice greatly in the Lord that at last you have renewed your concern for me. Indeed, you have been concerned, but you had no opportunity to show it. I am not saying this because I am

*in need, for I have learned to be content whatever the circum-
stances. I know what it is to be in need, and I know what it is to
have plenty. I have learned the secret of being content in any and
every situation, whether well fed or hungry, whether living in
plenty or in want. I can do everything through him who gives me
strength.*

*Yet it was good of you to share in my troubles. Moreover, as
you Philippians know, in the early days of your acquaintance
with the gospel, when I set out from Macedonia, not one church
shared with me in respect to giving and receiving, except you
only; for even when I was in Thessalonica, you sent me aid again
and again when I was in need. Not that I am looking for a gift,
but I am looking for what may be credited to your account. I
have received full payment and even more; I am amply supplied,
now that I have received from Epaphroditus the gifts you sent.
They are a fragrant offering, an acceptable sacrifice, pleasing to
God. And my God will meet all your needs according to his
glorious riches in Christ Jesus.*

To our God and Father be glory for ever and ever. Amen.

*Greet all the saints in Christ Jesus. The brothers who are with
me send greetings. All the saints send you greetings, especially
those who belong to Caesar's household.*

The grace of the Lord Jesus Christ be with your spirit.

WITH THAT, the old man was up on his feet
doing a dance on those old legs. In a sense it
was comical, yet Epaphroditus knew that it
was not a performance but something that came from the
heart. As he danced before the Lord, Paul went on
dictating, a little breathlessly: '*Rejoice in the Lord always. I
will say it again: Rejoice! Let your gentleness be evident to all.*'

'*All*, Paul!'

'Yes, all, and especially non-Christians. It's so easy to
rejoice among believers. The challenge is to do it before
all men, just like Stephen did. Oh, how I hated him for
that! So put it down, man, put it down: *The Lord is near*.
He is always in your hearts by his Holy Spirit to enable

you to do that. *Do not be anxious about anything, but in everything, by prayer and petition, with thanksgiving, present your requests to God. And the peace of God, which transcends all understanding...* Have you experienced that, Epaphroditus?'

'What do you mean?'

'Well, there are times when my old sinfulness rears its ugly head. I go ahead in my stubbornness and sin again, and when I feel certain that the Lord should punish me, instead he is ever merciful, gives me the opposite and goes on loving me. I sometimes want to be punished and wish he would take his peace away from me, but he doesn't. I can never understand that quality of love.'

'Neither can I.'

'Go on then: ...*will guard your hearts and your minds in Christ Jesus. Finally, brothers...*'

'You said that over an hour ago, Paul!'

'Did I? So I did. Never mind, this time I mean it...*Finally, brothers, whatever is true, whatever is noble, whatever is right, whatever is pure, whatever is lovely, whatever is admirable—if anything is excellent or praiseworthy—think about such things. Whatever you have learned or received or heard from me, or seen in me—put it into practice. And the God of peace will be with you. I rejoice greatly in the Lord that at last you have renewed your concern for me. Indeed, you have been concerned, but you had no opportunity to show it. I am not saying this because I am in need, for I have learned to be content whatever the circumstances.*'

'Are you really content at this moment, Paul? Especially since you don't know what awaits you from moment to moment?'

'Yes, hard as it is for you to understand that, my son, it's true. And I want them to know that, so that no matter what happens to me they won't be sorry. Say: *I know what it is to be in need, and I know what it is to have plenty.*

I have learned the secret of being content in any and every situation, whether well fed or hungry, whether living in plenty or in want. I can do everything through him who gives me strength.'

'Are you now saying that the Lord *does* want you to do everything and gives you the strength to do it?' cried Epaphroditus in exasperation.

'Listen to me carefully, my son,' replied Paul, placing his hand on his friend's shoulder. 'I'm saying that the Lord supplies the strength I need to do everything that *he* has inspired or commanded me to do, and everything I've talked about in this letter. Strength to be hungry, strength to encourage, strength to suffer, strength to intercede, strength to be lonely, strength to be poor, strength to be no longer up front, and strength to rejoice, no matter what. So often people think that having the Lord's strength is to get you away from all the negative and painful aspects of life. No, not at all. It reminds me of when Barnabas and I were encouraging the disciples in Lystra, Iconium and Antioch. We told them that we must all go through many hardships to enter the kingdom of God.[130] Jesus himself told his disciples that in this world they would have trouble. Praise God that he also pointed out that he had overcome the world!'[131]

'Funny how we so often hear God's word in the way we want to hear it, so that we can have a good time, as though we were entitled to years of happiness without problems.'

'Come on, Epaphroditus, it's getting late. Let's finish this.'

'Why the hurry now? Are you going somewhere?'

'I'm always going somewhere. Put down: *Yet it was good of you to share in my troubles. Moreover, as you Philippians know, in the early days of your acquaintance with the gospel, when I set out from Macedonia, not one church shared with me in respect to giving and receiving, except you only; for even when I was in Thessalonica, you sent me aid again and again when I was in need. Not that I am looking for a gift, but I am looking for what may be credited to your account. I have received full payment and even more; I am amply supplied, now that I have received from Epaphroditus the gifts you sent. They are a fragrant offering, an acceptable sacrifice, pleasing to God. And my God will meet all your needs according to his glorious riches in Christ Jesus. To our God and Father be glory for ever and ever. Amen.*

'Now end it with the usual type of farewell greeting. Say: *Greet all the saints in Christ Jesus. The brothers who are with me send greetings. All the saints send you greetings, especially those who belong to Caesar's household. The grace of the Lord Jesus Christ be with your spirit.* Amen.'

With that he gave a great sigh and sat down. Epaphroditus had some of Paul's last words running through his mind as he rounded off the letter. He could hear the voice of the old apostle, inside his head, saying majestically, 'But I have all, and abound: I am full...'[132]

He looked round the cell and wondered how Paul dared to say that. His belongings were all there and you would not have given a penny for some of them. He was sitting in well-worn clothes, sandals with a hole in the sole, and was beginning to shiver in the night air. He thought to himself, 'That's a fullness most Christians have never tasted...', and one more word shot through his mind; 'yet'. He put the pen down and began to roll up the parchment, ready for a good night's rest.

Dear Reader

To whom do you display your joy?

What do you spend your spare time thinking about?

Do you know how to remain content?

Is God your supplier of needs or wants?

Notes

130. Acts 14:22.
131. John 16:33.
132. Phil. 4:18, KJV.

Epilogue

As EPAPHRODITUS tidied away the ink-pot and pens and began to think about an evening meal he became aware of Paul scuffling around behind him. He turned to find the apostle on his knees feeling underneath the planking that served as a bed.

'What are you doing down there, Paul? Can I help?'

'I'm trying to find an old box that's got a weather-proof leather cover with thongs in it. You can use it to wrap up that scroll, to keep it clean and dry until you get it to Philippi.'

'Why the hurry? Can't that wait until tomorrow? We've done enough for today.'

'No, I need it now.'

Epaphroditus, thinking that tiredness was beginning to tell on Paul's temper, felt it better to humour the old man by getting it for him, if it would make him happy and settle him down.

'Here, let me find it for you.'

With that he brought out several items and finally the sought-after box. Paul rummaged round in it and found what he was looking for. Taking the scroll, he wrapped it up carefully, tied the thongs and, turning to his friend, handed it to him, saying, 'I want you to take it personally to Philippi.'

'I will, but first an evening meal.'

'No! You don't understand me, my son; I want you to take it now—tonight.'

Epaphroditus looked at him with astonishment.

'Now? Tonight?'

'Yes, tonight.'

Before he could put up any protest Paul went on: 'We've had a great day together, a day that will always be a favourite memory of mine, but I want you to do this for me now, even if you don't understand it. One day you might.'

Taking a little bag of money that he had stored away safely, he gave it to his friend and explained that it would see him safely on his journey and give him what he needed by way of food and shelter until he was home. Epaphroditus wanted to protest but already Paul was leading him to the cell door, crying for those wretched keys to come in the hand of the jailer to let his friend out. The jailer duly arrived and opened the door.

Epaphroditus and Paul stood facing each other; no more words were necessary. They took each other in their arms and hugged until they were both about to burst. For once, neither could find words to pray or to speak, nor did they even say goodbye. It was a holy moment, as though the Lord himself were there, saying that Christians never say goodbye for they are always in each other's hearts. Finally they broke from each other and with tears, whether of sorrow or joy one could not tell, they parted. The cell door closed between them, the key was turned and the steps of Epaphroditus and the jailer went off into the distance.

With renewed energy the old man crossed the room and began to move the table directly under the tiny

window, which was high up on the wall. He then shoved
and dragged the heavy bench over and began the
arduous task of getting himself up on to the table. Having achieved his goal, he grabbed the bars of the window
with both hands and pushed his face hard up against
them, as though he wanted to put his head straight
through them in order to lean out. In this precarious
position he watched and waited.

His waiting was rewarded, for there on the path that
led from the prison gate and down the road that would
lead him eventually to Philippi, he saw Epaphroditus
striding out, the leather-bound scroll held tightly under
his arm. His brother never even looked back. Paul
remained there until he disappeared from sight.

He was so caught up in watching Epaphroditus go, so
full of that moment, that he was completely oblivious to
the fact that the cell door had been opened and that it
was not the evening meal arriving, but several guards.
He suddenly had that feeling that something was happening behind him. Slowly turning round, almost like
Caesar on a throne towering over the guards, he stood
there majestically eyeing them. He caught sight of the
chains, and saw too that the guards were armed. With a
dignity possible only because of the presence and power
of Christ within his life, he said, 'I take it that the time
has come!'

They looked at him, amazed at his calmness, which
seemed to root them to the spot. Paul broke the silence
again. 'Would you be so good as to help me down?'

Two guards proceeded to help him off the table and
then all moved in close. The guard who was holding the
chains stepped forward but Paul simply looked at him
and said, 'They will not be necessary.'

To their amazement, he marched between them down
the corridor, without so much as a backward glance at

the cell, and out into the small square, where a group of officials had already assembled. Their task was to keep the legal documentation up to date with the final details of the execution of this innocent old man.

Paul walked to the dais and mounted the steps, never faltering, and knelt down. He was about to place his head on the block when a soldier came forward with a blindfold to put over his eyes.

'Kindly don't do that. With what eyesight I have left, I wish my last moments to be spent looking up.'

At that the soldier withdrew with a shrug and Paul placed his head on the block. Looking up as much as such a position would allow, he heard himself saying within, 'Maybe I, too, at the point of martyrdom, will see a vision of the glory of God and Jesus standing at the right hand of God!'[133]

Sure enough, those eyes of his, with a clarity he had not had in years, suddenly saw a figure appear in the distance, walking towards him with outstretched hands. He stared at those hands but, to his puzzlement, he could see no marks on them, no print of the nails. Looking up from the hands, he gazed straight into the smiling eyes of Stephen.

'Stephen! You! You're the last person I would have expected in a vision—you coming to meet me.'

'I've come to welcome you home and to escort you into the Lord's presence, my dear brother.'

'Then I hope they hurry up and get it over with, so that this vision can turn to reality.'

Stephen laughed.

'This *is* real, Paul. I'm no vision; you're home. The execution is over. You've left your earthly body, for as soon as your head touched the block, the axe descended.'

'But I felt nothing!'

'Why should that surprise you? Did you not, time and again in your preaching, assure Christians that they were not to fear death? Don't you remember writing, "Where, O death, is your victory? Where, O death, is your sting?"[134] Then you said it: now experience it. Come, let us go and see our Lord Jesus Christ.'

And with that, these two eternally youthful Spirit-bonded friends, arm in arm, walked away down a timeless pathway to be with the Lord for evermore.

Dear Reader

May I suggest that you now prayerfully read Paul's epistle to the Philippians straight through from start to finish. Hold up the mirror of God's word to your own life and situation; consider carefully how Paul spent his time in isolation. Ask the Lord to enable you, by his Spirit, to bring forth the fruit that he wants you to bear. Then, above all else, go out into life knowing you are walking towards a beginning and not an end.

Notes

133. Acts 7:55.
134. 1 Cor. 15:55.